M000289056

Everlasting Rain of Nectar

Everlasting Rain of Nectar

PURIFICATION PRACTICE IN TIBETAN BUDDHISM

Geshe Jampa Gyatso

Edited by Joan Nicell

Foreword by Lama Zopa Rinpoche

INCLUDING

A Significant Sight: A Commentary to the Bodhisattva's Confession of Downfalls
by Sanggye Yeshe
translated and edited by Joan Nicell

AND

The Bodhisattva's Confession of Downfalls
translated by George Churinoff

Wisdom Publications • Boston

WISDOM PUBLICATIONS
361 Newbury Street
Boston, Massachusetts 02115
United States of America

© 1996 Geshe Jampa Gyatso and Istituto Lama Tzong Khapa
© 1996 Joan Nicell, English translation of *A Significant Sight*
© 1996 George Churinoff, English translation of *The Bodhisattva's Confession of Downfalls*

All Rights Reserved.
No part of this book may be reproduced in any form or by any means, electronic or mechanical,
including photocopying, recording, or by any information storage and retrieval system or technologies now
known or later developed, without permission in writing from the publisher.

Library of Congress Cataloging-in-Publication Data
Jampa Gyatso, Geshe, 1932–
    Everlasting rain of nectar : purification practice in Tibetan Buddhism / Geshe Jampa Gyatso ;
    edited by Joan Nicell ; foreword by Lama Zopa Rinpoche ; including A significant sight : a
    commentary to the Bodhisattva's confession of downfalls by Sanggye Yeshe, translated and edited
    by Joan Nicell, and the Bodhisattva's confession of downfalls translated by George Churinoff.
        p.   cm.
    Includes bibliographical references.
    ISBN 0-86171-106-8 (alk. paper)
    1. Byan chub sems dpa'i ltun bśags. 2. Sans-rgyas-ye-śes, Mkhas-grub, 1525–1591.
Ltun ba bśags pa'i ṭikka. 3. Confession (Prayer)—Buddhism. 4. Atonement (Prayer)—
Buddhism. 5. Spiritual life—Buddhism. I. Nicell, Joan. II. Churinoff, George. III. Sans-
rgyas-ye-śes, Mkhas-grub, 1525–1591. Ltun ba bśags pa'i ṭikka. English. IV. Byan chub sems
dpa'i ltun bśags. English. V. Title.
BQ5594.C65B93335   1996
294.3'4446—dc20   95–43428

ISBN 0 86171 106 8

01 00 99 98 97
6   5   4   3   2

Designed by: LJ·SAWLit

Cover Art: Thirty-five Confessional Buddhas thangka, courtesy of University Museum of Zurich.
    [Mudras are thought to be according to a Nyingma visualization lineage for this practice.]
Line drawings: pp. 121–125, by Peter Iseli, Bern, Switzerland.

Typeset by Jason Fairchild in Goudy, Adobe Garamond, and Diacritical Garamond.

Wisdom Publications' books are printed on acid-free paper and meet the guidelines for permanence and durability
of the Committee on Production Guidelines for Book Longevity of the Council on Library Resources.

Printed in the United States of America.

Contents

Foreword

Students, all my brothers and sisters in the Dharma, this book contains *The Bodhisattva's Confession of Downfalls*, a practice for purifying negativities and downfalls, together with a commentary by Geshe Jampa Gyatso. Geshe-la is a highly qualified virtuous friend who possesses the three most important qualities of merit, warm heart, and pure morality. He has been teaching Dharma for many years in the West, particularly in Italy, and has been extremely kind to innumerable Westerners.

When we have enough merit, we will be able to understand the reasons why the practice of the Confession of Downfalls should be done by everyone who wants happiness and does not want suffering. Success in achieving happiness and avoiding problems, both now and in the future, depends upon two requisites. These requisites function whether we believe in them or not. For example, we might not believe that a particular tiny seed planted in the ground can grow into a tree with thousands of branches covered in leaves, so huge that it can provide shade for five hundred horse carriages; however, that does not mean that this tree does not exist. In fact, there is such a tree in India, the nayatoda tree. Likewise, even though we may not believe in reincarnation and the law of action and result, nor believe that this practice purifies our negativities, frees us from obstacles to generating the realizations of the path to enlightenment, frees us from the problems of this life and future lives, such as obstacles, illnesses, disharmony, harm, bad treatment, and abuse by others, and brings happiness and peace, both worldly and ultimate, it does not signify that this practice does not function to do so. Similarly, if we were to explain to a primitive person about rockets going to the moon, or about television, although he may not believe in the existence of these things, the mere fact that he does not believe in them does not mean that they do not exist. Reality is not necessarily as we believe it to be.

One of the requisites for success in achieving happiness and avoiding problems is to purify the causes of suffering, negativities created in the past.

However, although this is of benefit, merely to purify them alone is not sufficient; we also need to stop committing negativities in the future, the second requisite for achieving happiness. We need to change our own mind and our own actions; otherwise, we would be like the elephant who goes into the water to wash only to emerge and once again lay down in the sand—there would never be an end to our purification practice. This is why the practice of the Confession of Downfalls (which is done in conjunction with the four opponent forces) includes the force of turning away from faults in the future, the determination to not commit a particular negative action again, i.e., henceforth, to live in morality. With these two requisites, the purification of negativities already committed and the abstention from committing them again, we can purify all obstacles to our happiness.

Why are we not able to perfectly work for the benefit of sentient beings, to free them from suffering and cause them to attain happiness, and, especially, to lead them to enlightenment? It is because we are sentient beings whose minds are obscured; if instead, we were enlightened beings, buddhas, we would not have any obscurations whatsoever in our mental continua and would be able to perfectly benefit others. Therefore, since the practice of purification enables us to purify negative actions, the obscurations that prevent us achieving the realizations of the path to enlightenment, it is extremely important. By engaging in it, we will be able to perfectly work to free sentient beings from the depthless ocean of suffering and lead them to happiness; the very purpose of our lives.

When we mindfully and correctly practice the Confession of Downfalls even once, it has the power to purify even very heavy negative actions, such as the five actions of immediate retribution. This is the reason why Lama Tsongkhapa performed many hundreds of thousands of prostrations in conjunction with the recitation of the names of the thirty-five buddhas. This practice is extremely powerful; in some texts it is said that just by reciting the first name, that of Guru Shakyamuni Buddha, eighty thousand eons of negativities are purified. In fact, the mere recitation of each of the names of the thirty-five buddhas has the power to purify many eons of different types of negative actions. When this practice is performed together with prostrations (even the mere folding of the hands together in front of a statue of Buddha), we accumulate inconceivable merit. Therefore, it would be a great loss if we were not to take advantage of this opportunity to do this practice.

In short, *The Bodhisattva's Confession of Downfalls*, the recitation of the names of the thirty-five buddhas, particularly when done in conjunction with prostrations, is an unbelievably powerful purification, and enables us to accumulate extensive merit.

May this book composed by Geshe Jampa Gyatso greatly benefit numberless sentient beings by enabling them to purify their minds and achieve full enlightenment as quickly as possible.

Lama Thubten Zopa Rinpoche

Editor's Acknowledgments

The translation of the text *A Significant Sight* was made possible only due to Geshe Jampa Gyatso's infinite patience in answering my seemingly never-ending questions.

I am also extremely grateful to Venerable George Churinoff (Gelong Thubten Tsultrim), who not only encouraged me to learn Tibetan and taught me how to read it, but also went over the entire Tibetan text with me, thereby allowing me to improve the translation and to correct inaccuracies that would otherwise have gone unnoticed. I am also deeply indebted to Ven. George for his permission to include his recent translation of *The Bodhisattva's Confession of Downfalls* in this publication.

I would also like to extend my sincere thanks to Acharya Ngawang Lodoe for the help that he gave me in translating some of the more difficult grammatical points in the Tibetan text as well as for his help in writing the biography of Sanggye Yeshe.

I am also indebted to Peter Iseli for taking time out from his busy schedule to provide the line drawing of Sanggye Yeshe and the beautiful illustrations of how to do prostrations.

In addition, I would also like to express my appreciation to Venerable Massimo Stordi (Gelong Thubten Tsognyi), the director of Istituto Lama Tzong Khapa, for supporting me at the institute during the period of my work on this project.

Last, but definitely not least, a big thank you to the staff of Wisdom Publications, in particular Venerable Connie Miller, Editorial Projects Manager, for their advice, encouragement, and patience during all stages of this work.

Publisher's Acknowledgments

The publisher thanks the Hershey Family Foundation, Chiu-Nan Lai, Fiorella Bonolis and Luigi Carpineti, Magda Cavalieri, Sante Cinti, Laura Coccitto, Istituto Lama Tzong Khapa, Joan Nicell, Tagden Shedrub Ling Monastery, and Thubten Tsognyi for their kindness in sponsoring the production of this book.

Preface

The practices of purifying negativities and accumulating merit are the heart of the many methods taught in the Buddhist sutra and tantra teachings for attaining enlightenment. To gain any mental, or spiritual, development whatsoever, it is absolutely necessary to purify the negativities of body, speech, and mind that we have accumulated throughout our beginningless lives. These negativities have left imprints on our mental continuum that at some future time will ripen in the experience of suffering. Therefore, to avoid rebirth in the lower realms and the experience of unhappiness in future lives, and to gain liberation and enlightenment, it is essential to purify our mental continuum.

In addition to purifying negativities, we need to accumulate merit, or positive energy, to achieve enlightenment. This is done by engaging in virtuous actions, such as the practice of the six perfections—generosity, morality, patience, joyous effort, concentration, and wisdom. By means of these practices a bodhisattva, a being who is striving to attain enlightenment, is able to accumulate the merit necessary to bring about the mental development that reaches its zenith in the state of complete omniscience.

The advantage of engaging in the practice of *The Bodhisattva's Confession of Downfalls* is that it enables us both to purify our negativities and to accumulate merit. By applying the four opponent forces, which counteract our negativities, we purify our mental continuum of negative energy; by rejoicing in all the virtues created by ourselves and others and dedicating them to unsurpassed enlightenment, we accumulate great stores of positive energy.

For these reasons, the practice of *The Bodhisattva's Confession of Downfalls* is an essential method enabling both beginners and advanced practitioners to achieve spiritual development. A well-known story illustrates the benefit of this practice: Lama Tsongkhapa himself engaged in extensive purification through reciting this sutra and performing one hundred thousand prostrations to each of the thirty-five tathāgatas—a total of three and a half million prostrations.

During the Easter weekend of 1993 Geshe Jampa Gyatso, the resident teacher at Istituto Lama Tzong Khapa, Pomaia, Italy, gave an oral commentary to *The Bodhisattva's Confession of Downfalls* based on the Tibetan commentary *A Significant Sight: A Commentary to the Bodhisattva's Confession of Downfalls* by Sanggye Yeshe. Prior to the course, I hurriedly produced an extremely rough translation that has subsequently been revised with much help from Geshe-la and George Churinoff. Since the practice of *The Bodhisattva's Confession of Downfalls* has enormous benefits, I hope that these two commentaries on the practice—one by a noted lineage guru of the lam-rim teachings and one by a contemporary teacher thoroughly familiar with the Western mind—will inspire many people to engage in this profound practice.

Joan Nicell (Getsulma Tenzin Chöden)

Technical Note

The root text, *The Bodhisattva's Confession of Downfalls*, translated by George Churinoff and included here with his kind permission, is set out in italic type to distinguish it from the commentary *A Significant Sight* by Sanggye Yeshe. Both the root text and Sanggye Yeshe's commentary have been indented to set them apart from Geshe Jampa Gyatso's explanations. I have abbreviated and modified some of the titles and subtitles in Sanggye Yeshe's commentary and have added extra subtitles at many points. A complete translation of the original outline can be found in the appendices.

For the sake of readability, phrases such as "This is taught (or shown) by saying...," or "The meaning of this is...," that occur in Sanggye Yeshe's commentary, respectively before and after each section of the root text, have been omitted. While these phrases are necessary in the Tibetan to show the demarcation between the root text, *The Bodhisattva's Confession of Downfalls*, and the author's commentary, I felt them to be unnecessary in the English as this demarcation has been accomplished typographically. Also, while the commentary generally cites only the first and last few words of each of the relevant sections of the root text, here complete citations have been included for easier reference.

The short biography of Sanggye Yeshe is a summary of the main points of the extensive biography found in Yeshe Gyeltsen's *Biographies of the Lineage Gurus of the Stages of the Path*.[1] The chart indicating the colors and hand positions of the thirty-five tathāgatas is translated from Lama Tsongkhapa's *Practice of the Thirty-five Buddhas and a Description of the Deities' Bodies.*

Most of the commentary by Geshe Jampa Gyatso included here is a transcription of his 1993 teachings on the text *A Significant Sight*. However, the detailed explanations of actions and their results—the four characteristics of actions (included in Geshe-la's *Introduction*), the four types of results (included in the chapter *The Four Opponent Forces*), and the four branches of a complete path of action, as well as the ten non-virtues (included in the chapter *The Force of Total Repudiation* under the sub-section *Negativities Included in the Ten Non-Virtues*)—have been incorporated from Geshe-la's teachings on *The Quick Path* (*nyur-lam*) given at Istituto Lama Tzong Khapa, August 2–8, 1984. The subsection *The Mind of Enlightenment* included in the chapter on *The Force of the Basis* is a transcription of Geshe-la's commentary, given at Istituto Lama Tzong Khapa during the weekend of February 23–24, 1985, on a text from *The Collected Works On Mind Training* by Kyabje Trijang Rinpoche. At Geshe-la's suggestion I myself wrote the very brief overview of the seven-point meditation for developing the mind of enlightenment. This is not included in a more detailed format since extensive explanations of this meditation are already available in other English commentaries on the stages of the path (*lam-rim*). The lists of the eight qualities of the Buddha, Dharma, and Sangha Jewels (included in the subsection *Refuge* in the chapter on *The Force of the Basis*) are an abbreviated translation from Jetsün Chökyi Gyeltsen's *Ocean Playground of the Lord of the Nāgas*. In addition, when I felt that a certain point needed further explanation, I personally questioned Geshe-la about it and then added his clarifications to this text.

Words already familiar to most Western Buddhist readers—including bodhisattva, buddha, daka, dakini, dharani, Dharma, guru, mantra, nirvana, sangha, stupa, sutra, and tantra—have been treated as English words throughout the text and consequently the Sanskrit diacritical marks have been omitted.

The transliteration of Sanskrit words is according to the standard international system except that for ease of reading in English ś is written as sh, ṣ as ṣh, c as ch, and ch as chh. The transliteration of the Tibetan follows the system of Turrell Wylie except that the root letter, rather than the initial letter, is capitalized in proper names and titles. However, I have written Tibetan proper names and the phonetics of *The Bodhisattva's Confession of Downfalls* in a very simple manner, preferring to facilitate their reading rather than striving for perfect pronunciation. Exceptions are the spelling of Tsongkhapa, which corresponds to the transliteration system, and the names of those contemporary Tibetans who already use a particular English spelling. The following chart shows the transliteration on the left and the phonetics on the right.

ka – ka	kha – ka	ga – ga	nga – nga
ca – cha	cha – cha	ja – ja	nya – nya
ta – ta	tha – ta	da – da	na – na
pa – pa	pha – pa	ba – ba	ma – ma
tsa – tza	tsha – tsa	dza – dza	wa – wa
zha – zha	za – za	'a– a	ya – ya
ra – ra	la – la	sha – sha	sa – sa
ha – ha	a – a		

A distinction is usually made between the phonetics of the first and second letters of the first through fourth lines of the alphabet, either by adding an apostrophe or an 'h' to the letters in the second column. Since this generally makes little difference to the resulting pronunciation for people unfamiliar with colloquial Tibetan, I have chosen the simplest mode for ease of reading and have not made any distinction. In addition, I have chosen to use 'e' instead of 'ä' since 'e' is more familiar to the native English speaker. Instead of 'äï', 'öï', and 'üï' I have used the simpler 'e', 'ö' and 'ü' since the pronunciation is very similar even though the 'ï' indicates a slight lengthening of the vowel sound.

Sanggye Yeshe (1525–1591)

A Short Biography of Sanggye Yeshe

Sanggye Yeshe was born in 1525 in the small village of Druggya in the Tsang valley of Tibet. Auspicious signs occurred at his birth and even at a very young age his behavior was uncommonly mature and subdued. He was often seen playing at teaching Dharma, meditating, and debating and, although very young, he often expressed the wish to become a monk. This behavior is attributed to his familiarity with the morality of renunciation, gained in many previous lives when he had been born as a learned scholar and yogi in India. The renowned Gyelwa Ensapa, considered by Tibetans to be the first Panchen Lama, foreseeing that Sanggye Yeshe was to become his successor as a lineage holder, urged the parents to take special care of their son.

At the age of ten, the young boy received lay vows (*upāsaka, dge bsnyen*)[2] from his first teacher, Yönten Zangpo, and was given the name Chökyab Dorje. He studied reading and writing with this teacher, demonstrating remarkable ease in understanding whatever he was taught. Later, upon receiving the vows of a novice monk (*shrāmaṇera, dge tsul*) from this same master, he became known as Sanggye Yeshe.

At the age of fifteen Sanggye Yeshe entered Tashilünpo Monastery and began studying the philosophical subjects with Tsöndru Gyeltsen. The following year, when considering the possibility of going to study at Sera Monastery with Jetsün Chökyi Gyeltsen, a friend advised him to study instead under the tutelage of that master's disciple, Jamyang Gendün Lozang, who was considered to be a manifestation of Manjushri. Sanggye Yeshe studied the *Pramāṇavārttika* teachings with this master and then returned to Tashilünpo Monastery, where until the age of eighteen he studied *Mādhyamika*. At the age of nineteen he debated in front of a large gathering of abbots and monks at Tashilünpo and, undefeated, became renowned for his knowledge and understanding of the scriptures.

Sanggye Yeshe then studied the *Pāramitās* and the *Vinaya* and once again his extraordinary depth of understanding was noted by his teachers. At the age of twenty-six, following the advice of Gendün Lozang, he became the disciplinarian at Tashilünpo. At the conclusion of these duties, Sanggye Yeshe traveled to Gangchen Chöpel Monastery where he received many teachings from Panchen Rinpoche Dönyö Gyeltsen on both sutra and tantra, including the transmission of many teachings on mind training (*lojong*). He then attended the Lower Tantric College, where he studied and mastered the tantras, rituals, ritual dance, mandala drawing, ritual music, chanting, and the rituals associated with burnt offerings. During this time a severe bout of leg pain made Sanggye Yeshe determine to return to Tsang following the completion of his studies at the Lower Tantric College. This pain is attributed to Palden Lhamo, a Dharma protector, who had been directed by Gyelwa Ensapa to bring Sanggye Yeshe back to him. Subsequently, Sanggye Yeshe went to study with Gyelwa Ensapa and received the transmission of the teachings on the stages of the path (lam-rim) from this learned master, who became his root guru. Sanggye Yeshe spent many years in meditation based on these teachings, greatly pleasing his teacher. Having requested Gyelwa Ensapa for permission to receive the vows of a fully ordained monk (*bhikshu, dge slong*), he received them from the abbot of Riwo Gepel Monastery, Chogle Nampar Gyelwa. After receiving teachings from this abbot, Sanggye Yeshe returned to Ensa Monastery where he received the transmission of a great number of tantra initiations and commentaries from Gyelwa Ensapa. Upon the passing away of this precious master, Sanggye Yeshe made many offerings to the monastery and commissioned the making of many images.

Twice Sanggye Yeshe became the abbot of Riwo Gepel Monastery and in this position turned the wheel of Dharma for the benefit of his many disciples. Later returning to Ensa, he gave extensive teachings on both the sutras and tantras. During this time, he took great care of Gyelwa Ensapa's incarnation, Lozang Chökyi Gyeltsen, bestowing upon him the lay and, later, the novice vows, as well as many teachings and the blessings of numerous initiations.

In short, Sanggye Yeshe's entire life was dedicated to Dharma practice—the suppressing of the mental afflictions and the practice of deity yoga. He passed away in 1591 at the age of sixty-seven, his death being accompanied by many marvelous signs. Various rites were conducted during the forty-nine days in which his body remained enclosed in a special structure built for the cremation. Following the cremation, uncommonly large relic pills, one the size of a pea, were found amassed together in the shape of eyes, brain, tongue, heart, and central channel. His main disciple, Panchen Lozang Chökyi Gyeltsen, had a stupa constructed on the cremation site to contain the relics and commissioned the making of a huge gold-covered copper statue of Sanggye Yeshe. It was upon the passing away of his precious root guru, Sanggye Yeshe, that Panchen Lozang Chökyi Gyeltsen was inspired to write *The Offering to the Guru* (*Guru Puja, Lama Chöpa*). Although Sanggye Yeshe had many well-known disciples, the best is said to have been Lozang Chökyi Gyeltsen, the reincarnation of Gyelwa Ensapa, who, although considered by Westerners to be the first Panchen Lama, is considered by Tibetans to be the second.

Introduction

by Geshe Jampa Gyatso

From a Buddhist point of view our experiences, pleasant and unpleasant, come about as a result of our own previous actions, virtuous and non-virtuous. These actions can be physical, verbal, or mental. However, in each of these cases the action originally stems from the mind since, prior to engaging in an action, a wish or intention to do that particular action always arises. Following upon the intention, we actually engage in the action. We experience its corresponding result later on, generally in a future life but possibly even in the same life. Since all our experiences are the result of our previous actions, the Buddha emphasized the law of cause and result in his teachings. For example, Buddha taught that actions have four general characteristics: (1) actions are definite, (2) actions increase, (3) actions not done will not be experienced, and (4) actions done will not go to waste.

1. Actions are definite

Virtuous actions definitely bring the result of happiness and never bring the result of suffering. Likewise, non-virtuous actions definitely bring the result of suffering and never bring the result of happiness. Internal causes and results function along much the same principles as external causes and results. An example of an external cause is planting an apple seed in the ground; in accordance with the cause, the apple seed, the result of an apple tree is produced. Instead, if we were to plant a pepper seed the result of a pepper plant would arise. An apple seed cannot give rise to a pepper plant nor can a pepper seed give rise to an apple tree. Internal causes and results function in the same manner; in accordance with the cause, virtuous actions, we definitely experience the result of happiness. Likewise, in accordance with the cause, non-virtuous actions, we definitely experience the result of suffering. Just as the small pleasure of a cool breeze on a hot day is the result of a past virtuous action, similarly, the small suffering of a thorn pricking the sole of our foot is the result of a past non-virtuous action.

2. Actions increase

In the same way that a tiny seed can produce the result of a huge tree, a very small virtuous or non-virtuous action can bring a great result. This is due to the fact that an action continues to increase as long as its antidote is not applied. If a non-virtuous action is purified using an appropriate method, even if we cannot completely avoid experiencing its result, at the very least we will be able to stop it from increasing. Similarly, it is possible to destroy our virtuous actions through becoming angry or developing wrong views.

3. Actions not done will not be experienced

Not having planted seeds in the ground, we will not reap a crop in the autumn. Likewise, if we have not done a particular virtuous or non-virtuous action, we will not experience its respective result of happiness or unhappiness.

4. Actions done will not go to waste

Having done a virtuous or non-virtuous action, if it is not destroyed by its antidote, it will bring its result when the necessary conditions come together. An action will never go to waste due to the passage of time. Just as when we put our money in a bank it is not used up as long as we do not withdraw it and, in the meantime, it continually produces interest; likewise, when we do an action, if it is not destroyed by its antidote, it will not go to waste but will continually increase.

In addition to explaining the detailed functioning of actions and results, the Buddha also explained, by way of his clairvoyant powers, why a particular person was experiencing certain problems. He often told how at one time such-and-such a person had taken such-and-such a birth, did such-and-such an action, and was thereby experiencing such-and-such a result. Many examples of these stories can be found in *The Sutra of One Hundred Actions* (*Karmashataka, mDo sde las brgya pa*) and *The Sutra of the Wise and the Foolish* (*Damamūko nāma sūtra, mDzangs blun zhe bya ba'i mdo*).

఍ ❈ ఍

Through understanding that virtuous actions bring happiness and non-virtuous actions bring suffering, we see how important it is to continually strive to develop a good motivation and to engage in virtuous actions. At the same time, we understand that we must completely abandon committing even seemingly insignificant non-virtuous actions so as to avoid experiencing further suffering and problems in the future. However, even though we may intellectually understand this, because our mind is not subdued and is therefore influenced by many types of negative emotions or afflictions, we continue to commit non-virtuous actions. Our negative emotions are very strong while our positive thoughts are generally quite weak; consequently, these two are always in competition. Most of the time the weaker positive side loses and the more powerful negative side wins. Thereby, our mind remains dominated by afflictions that in turn cause us to engage in non-virtuous physical and verbal actions. Therefore, just as to clean our dirty clothes we wash them with soap and water, in a similar way we need to wash, or purify, our mental continuum of non-virtuous actions of body, speech, and mind. To avoid experiencing their unpleasant results it is extremely important that we develop the habit of regularly purifying our inner dirt, the impure mind. For this purpose we need to engage in a practice of purification such as *The Bodhisattva's Confession of Downfalls*. When this practice is done in conjunction with the application of the four opponent forces, not only will we purify the non-virtuous actions committed in this life, we will also purify those committed during all our beginningless lives in cyclic existence. Therefore, this practice is of extreme importance in our quest for spiritual, or mental, development.

The Text

A Significant Sight: A Commentary to the Bodhisattva's Confession of Downfalls

*Byang chub sems dpa'i ltung ba bshags pa'i tikka
don ldan ces bya ba bzhugs*

by Sanggye Yeshe

with commentary by Geshe Jampa Gyatso

Introduction

by Sanggye Yeshe

> I devoutly prostrate to the thirty-five tathāgatas, the gurus, the special
> deities, and all those worthy of prostration.

AT THE BEGINNING of his commentary, Sanggye Yeshe pays homage, or
prostrates, to the thirty-five tathāgatas, the gurus, the special deities, and all
those worthy of prostration. Tathāgata, a Sanskrit epithet for a buddha, literally translated as One Gone Thus, indicates that a buddha simultaneously
knows all phenomena as well as their thusness, or emptiness. "Guru" in
Sanskrit, "lama" in Tibetan, "spiritual teacher" in English, refer to both the
teachers from whom we directly receive teachings as well as to the lineage
gurus from whom we indirectly receive teachings. The syllable *gu* of guru
derives from the Sanskrit word *gun*, meaning "quality," while *ru* derives
from *rup*, meaning "heavy" or "weighty." Therefore, the Sanskrit word *guru*
signifies "one with weighty qualities."

In the context of Buddhism there are four classes of tantra: action, perfor-
mance, yoga, and highest yoga tantra. The deities of these four classes are
called special deities. Four special, or main, deities are practiced in the
Kadampa tradition: Shākyamuni Buddha, Avalokiteshvara (Chenrezig
Wangchug), Tārā (Drolma), and Achala (Miyowa). Shākyamuni Buddha is
the founder of the doctrine; Avalokiteshvara is the compassion of all the
buddhas of the three times manifested as a deity; Tārā is the manifestation of
all the buddhas' activities; and Achala is the manifestation of all the buddhas'
energy or power. By practicing these four deities we are able to make rapid
progress in our spiritual, or mental, development.

"All those worthy of prostration" refers to the objects of prostration: the
buddhas, bodhisattvas, solitary realizers (*pratyekabuddha, rang sangs rgyas*),
earers *(shrāvaka, nyan thos)*, dakas, dakinis *(ḍāka/ḍākiṇī, mkha' 'gro/ma*, sky-

goer),[3] and Dharma protectors (*dharmapāla, chos skyong*).[4] Prostrations are a way of showing respect for the objects we venerate. The Tibetan word for prostration is *chag-tsel* (*abhivandana, phyag 'tshal*) with the particle *lo* being added to show the end of the phrase. Although *chag* in most contexts is the honorific word for "hand," here, in relation to the objects of prostration, it means, "You who possess the qualities of perfect compassion, wisdom, skill, and so on." *Tsel* means "to desire"; in this context, "I desire to attain your realizations." Here *lo* signifies, "Please bestow on me your realizations."

Prostrations are performed with the body, speech, and mind. We prostrate with our body by touching our legs, arms, and head to the ground; with our speech by reciting verses of praise; and with our mind by generating faith through remembering and rejoicing in the qualities of the objects of prostration.

> I will express a mere portion of the meaning of the profound *Sutra of the Bodhisattva's Confession of Downfalls* (*byang chub sems dpa'i ltung ba bshags pa yi mdo sde*).

The author of the commentary promises to give a short explanation of *The Sutra of the Bodhisattva's Confession of Downfalls* in a very simple way that is easy to understand.

> Our unsurpassed teacher, lord of the subduers, taught us, the disciples of the three realms, eighty-four thousand collections of doctrine as antidotes to be used against the eighty-four thousand afflictions (*klesha, nyon mongs*)—attachment and so forth.

The teachings of Shākyamuni Buddha are said to be able to subdue the disciples of the three realms, the beings of the desire, form, and formless realms. However, there is some debate as to whether or not the beings of the formless realm can actually be Shākyamuni Buddha's disciples since lacking the aggregate of form they do not have sense faculties and, consequently, can neither see Buddha nor listen to his teachings. The conclusion is that Buddha's disciples do in fact exist in the formless realm since a superior (*ārya, 'phags pa*)[5] who was Buddha's disciple in a previous life can be reborn there.

There is a total of eighty-four thousand afflictions because there exist twenty-one thousand types of attachment, anger, and ignorance, respectively, as well as twenty-one thousand afflictions that are a combination of the three. Buddha gave his teachings, the eighty-four thousand collections of doctrine, as the antidotes to corresponding afflictions in accordance with the various dispositions, interests, and thoughts of the many sentient beings.

> In the profound *Sutra Indicating the Four Dharmas* (*Ārya chaturdhar-manirdesha nāma mahāyāna sūtra, 'Phags pa chos bzhi bstan pa zhes bya ba theg pa chen po'i mdo*), which is like the foundation, or base, and root of the [eighty-four thousand collections of doctrine], it is taught, "Furthermore, when a non-virtuous action (*karma, las*) is performed, the function of total repudiation is to develop regret for it."

The four dharmas are the four opponent forces, the four essential aspects of every purification practice. The sutra that explains them is called the foundation, base, and root of the eighty-four thousand collections of doctrine, all Buddha's teachings, because these antidotes to the eighty-four thousand afflictions can be subsumed in the four opponent forces which are the means to purify all negativities.

> The meaning of this [quotation] is explained in the *Compendium of Instructions* (*Shikṣhāsamuchchaya, bsLab pa kun las btus pa*) through dividing [the explanation] into two: (1) the confession of the heap of negativities in general, and (2) the confession of the downfalls of a bodhisattva in particular.

Heap, or aggregate, implies many things brought together; in this case, our non-virtuous actions. Shāntideva in his *Compendium of Instructions* explains how, in general, to purify the many negative actions we have committed in both this and previous lives, as well as explaining how, in particular, to purify those committed by a bodhisattva. Although the term "bodhisattva" (*bodhisattva, byang chub sems dpa'*) usually specifically refers to a being who has actually generated the mind of enlightenment (*bodhichitta, byang chub kyi sems*), here in this context it includes any person who even aspires to develop the wish to attain enlightenment for the sake of all sentient beings.

Furthermore, four confessions of downfalls are taught in *The Heap of Jewels Sutra* (*Ārya mahāratnakūṭadharma-paryāyashatasāhasrikagrantha sūtra*, *'Phags pa dkon mchog brtsegs pa chen po'i chos kyi rnam grangs le'u stong phrag brgya pa'i mdo*), the delineation of the vinaya (*'dul ba*, discipline) requested by Upali: (1) confession to a group of ten, (2) confession to a group of five, and (3) confession in front of one or two—these being from the point of view of the gravity of the downfall—and (4) confession in the presence of the thirty-five buddhas. Amongst them, the topic on this occasion is the sutra taught to show how to confess negativities and downfalls before the thirty-five buddhas.

As taught in *The Heap of Jewels Sutra*, downfalls are confessed in front of larger or smaller groups of fully ordained monks in dependence on the gravity of the downfall. We should confess our heavier, or more serious, downfalls before a group of ten monks, our lesser downfalls before a group of five, and our least serious transgressions before one or two monks. Alternatively, we can confess our negativities in the presence of the thirty-five buddhas through reciting *The Sutra of the Bodhisattva's Confession of Downfalls* in conjunction with performing prostrations. The explanation of the latter method for confessing downfalls is the topic of this commentary.

Part One

Purifying Negativities and Downfalls

1

The Four Opponent Forces

As taught, "Especially due to the importance of purifying karmic obscurations, continually cherish reliance on all four forces," it is necessary to confess negativities and downfalls by means of all four opponent forces.

This quotation from Lama Tsongkhapa's *Lines of Experience* (*Nyams mgur*) emphasizes the importance of purifying our negativities and downfalls through applying all four opponent forces. The term "negativity" (*papa, sdig pa*) includes all non-virtuous actions of body, speech, and mind. The term "downfall" (*apatti, ltung ba*), also sometimes translated as transgression, literally means to fall down, signifying that the result of this type of action is to fall down into the lower realms, i.e., to be reborn there in the future. Although all non-virtuous actions are downfalls, the term particularly refers to actions that involve the transgression of a vow, which may or may not be non-virtuous. A transgression of a vow is non-virtuous if it involves committing a natural misdeed (*prakṛti-sāvadya, rang bzhin gyi kha na ma tho ba*) (e.g., transgressing the vow to abandon killing) or a formulated misdeed (*pratikṣhepaṇa-sāvadya, bcas pa'i kha na ma tho ba*) (e.g., transgressing the vow to abandon dancing) accompanied by an attitude of contempt for the vow. Examples of these non-virtues are, respectively, a person with individual liberation vows killing a sentient being and a fully ordained monk dancing with the thought that it does not matter that he has a vow to abandon dancing. However, if a monk dances with the motivation of benefiting others, although he would commit a downfall, it would not become a non-virtuous action.

The four opponent forces are (1) the force of the basis, (2) the force of applying all antidotes, (3) the force of total repudiation, and (4) the force of turning away from faults in the future. The force of the basis includes both going for refuge to the Buddha, Dharma, and Sangha, and generating the mind of enlightenment in order to benefit sentient beings. Thus, the first opponent force is completed with the generation of these two minds.

The force of applying all antidotes means to apply one of the six types of antidotes as a countermeasure to purify our negativities and downfalls. The six antidotes are (1) recitation of sutras, (2) meditation on emptiness, (3) recitation of mantras[6] such as the hundred-syllable mantra of Vajrasattva, (4) making or commissioning statues or paintings of the buddhas, (5) making offerings to buddhas or stupas (*stūpa, mchod rten,* reliquary monument),[7] and (6) recitation of the names of buddhas such as the thirty-five tathāgatas. However, in addition to these, any positive action done with the purpose of purifying can become an antidote to the imprints left on our mental continuum by the negative actions we have committed.

The force of total repudiation is the generation of a deep sense of regret for the negative actions we have done. Accepting or acknowledging that a mistaken action was our own fault is one way of demonstrating this regret.

The force of turning away from faults in the future means to strongly determine, or resolve, not to do, or at least to try not to do, a negative action again. Through making such a firm determination we will eventually be able to completely stop engaging in that particular action.

When each of these four opponent forces is present in our confession we can totally purify our negative actions. However, if our purification lacks even one of them it will not be completely effective since each of the forces acts as a specific antidote to the four results that arise from a complete path of action. These are (1) the maturation result, (2) the result corresponding to the cause as an experience, (3) the result corresponding to the cause as an activity, and (4) the environmental result. Having committed a non-virtuous action such as killing, our maturation result is a future rebirth in one of the three lower realms as a hell being, hungry ghost, or animal—this is purified by the force of applying all antidotes. The result corresponding to the cause as an experience is the experience of suffering and difficulties when we are once again reborn as a human; for example, as a result of having killed, our life will be short and we will experience many illnesses—this is purified by the force of total repudiation. The result corresponding to the cause as an activity is that when once again reborn as a human we will spontaneously engage in that specific non-virtuous action due to our previous familiarity with it; for example, due to having killed in a past life we will engage in killing or torturing insects and small animals even as a young child—this is purified by the force of turning away from faults in the future. The environmental result refers to the particular physical environment in which we take rebirth as a human; for example, the environmental result of killing is rebirth in a place where food and medicines are either of poor quality or difficult to obtain—this is purified by the force of the basis. Similarly, the other nine non-virtuous paths of action when complete produce the four types of result.[8] Therefore, to purify all four results of our negativities it is of utmost importance to include each of the four opponent forces in our purification practice.

Lama Tsongkhapa also stressed the need to continually purify our negativities and downfalls since we continually engage in committing them. It is not at all sufficient to confess them merely once a year, or even once a month.

2

The Force of the Basis

I go for refuge to the Buddha.
I go for refuge to the Dharma.
I go for refuge to the Sangha.

The force of the basis is going for refuge from the depths of our hearts
to the Three Jewels, the Buddha and so on, for the purpose of cleansing
and purifying our negativities and downfalls, by means of reflecting
that they know all our negativities and downfalls.

Even though I should explain the individual identification of the
refuges, how to go for refuge, and so forth, I will not write about this
here as it would be too long.

Although going for refuge to the guru is included in the refuge verse of
the root text it is not mentioned here in the commentary. Going for refuge
to the Three Jewels—the Buddha, Dharma, and Sangha—and generating
the wish to attain enlightenment to benefit all sentient beings comprises the
first opponent force, the force of the basis. It is called the force of the basis
because our collection of virtuous, non-virtuous, and unpredicted, or neutral, actions are committed with respect to either of two referent objects,
the Three Jewels or sentient beings. In turn we need to rely upon them to
purify our non-virtuous actions. By going for refuge to the Three Jewels we
purify negativities committed in relation to them, and by generating the
wish to attain enlightenment we purify negativities committed in relation
to sentient beings. Just as when we fall down on the ground, the ground
itself acts as our basis, or support, for being able to stand up again; likewise,
when we commit negative actions against the Three Jewels and sentient
beings, they themselves act as the basis of our purification. For this reason

we rely on the force of the basis—refuge and the mind of enlightenment—
to purify our negativities.

1) REFUGE

Identifying the Three Jewels

Explained very simply the actual Buddha Jewel is any omniscient being such
as Shākyamuni Buddha who has abandoned all faults and achieved all realizations. More precisely the actual Buddha Jewel is the final object of refuge
that possesses the eight qualities of being uncompounded and so forth (see
below). It includes the four bodies of a buddha: the nature body
(*svabhāvikakāya, ngo bo nyid sku*), truth body (*dharmakāya, chos sku*), enjoyment body (*saṃbhogakāya, longs sku*), and emanation body (*nirmāṇakāya,
sprul sku*).[9] The Buddha Jewel also encompasses the body, speech, and mind
of a buddha—the results of a bodhisattva's collection of merit and wisdom
over three countless great eons. The conventional Buddha Jewel is any representation of a buddha, such as a statue or painting.

The actual Dharma Jewel is any true path or true cessation; respectively, the
method to abandon an object of abandonment and the abandonment itself.
The conventional Dharma Jewel is any text or book of the Buddha's teachings.

The actual Sangha Jewel is any single person who has attained the path of
seeing (i.e., has directly realized emptiness) and is thereby a superior. Thus,
the Sangha Jewel is those beings who have acquired the realizations of true
paths and true cessations, the real Dharma Jewel, in their mental continuum. The conventional Sangha Jewel is a group of four or more fully
ordained monks or nuns.

The meaning of Buddha, Dharma, and Sangha can be more easily understood by making a simple illustration. We ourselves can be likened to university students, the Buddha to our professor, the Dharma to the subject matter,
and the Sangha to our classmates. The professor, having already mastered a
particular subject, teaches us according to his or her own knowledge and
experience; similarly, the buddhas teach us the path to enlightenment based
on their own knowledge and experience of it. When we study a particular
subject well we gain some knowledge concerning it, this knowledge is com-
parable to the Dharma Jewel, the knowledge that actually protects us from
suffering and problems. While at university we rely upon our classmates and

friends for help and support; likewise, the Sangha are the virtuous friends who help us to attain buddhahood. Through putting effort into learning the subject that the professor teaches us, we ourselves can become university teachers; correspondingly, through studying, meditating, and correctly practicing the Dharma that was taught by the Buddha, we ourselves can become buddhas. Reflection on this simple illustration can help us to understand the significance of the Three Jewels and thereby deepen our practice of taking refuge.

The Qualities of the Three Jewels

To develop stable faith, confidence, and appreciation that Buddha, Dharma, and Sangha are in fact valid objects of refuge we need to deepen our knowledge concerning their individual qualities. Having done this, when we recite the refuge verse and simultaneously remember and reflect on the particular qualities of each of the Three Jewels, the practice of taking refuge will be much more effective since it will come from our heart.

The qualities of the Buddha Jewel can be subdivided into the qualities of a buddha's body, speech, and mind. In brief, the inconceivable qualities of a buddha's body are manifested in the thirty-two major marks and eighty minor marks with which it is adorned, each of which is a result of having collected its respective cause.[10]

The melodious speech of a buddha has sixty-four qualities.[11] Due to its power even a single word is heard and understood in accordance with the dispositions, interests, and thoughts of the various listeners. For example, once when Shākyamuni Buddha said the I is impermanent, one disciple heard the I is suffering, another the I is empty, and another the I is selfless. Simultaneously, due to the power of Buddha's speech, these disciples each heard a different teaching appropriate to their own particular level of spiritual development.

A buddha's mind has many inconceivable qualities; for example, the twenty-one divisions of uncontaminated exalted wisdom that include the divisions of the ten strengths, the four fearlessnesses, the four individual knowledges, the eighteen unique qualities, and so forth.[12]

❧ ❧ ❧

Eight qualities of each of the Three Jewels are further elaborated in Maitreya's *Sublime Continuum of the Great Vehicle* (*Mahāyāna-uttara-tantra-shāstra, Theg pa chen po rgyud bla ma'i bstan bcos*).

The Buddha Jewel has the eight qualities of
1. uncompoundedness
2. spontaneously and effortlessly accomplishing all
3. inconceivability and inexpressibility
4. knowledge of ultimate and conventional truths
5. mercy
6. ability
7. [fulfillment of] the welfare of self
8. [fulfillment of] the welfare of others

The Dharma Jewel has the eight qualities of being
1. unimaginable
2. without the two, contaminated actions and afflictions
3. free from conceptualization
4. pure
5. clear
6. an antidote
7. true cessations
8. true paths

The Sangha Jewel has the eight qualities of
1. conventional knowledge
2. ultimate knowledge
3. inner knowledge (i.e., knowledge of the five sciences—medicine, literature, arts, dialectics, and philosophy)
4. being purified of obscurations of attachment (i.e., afflictive obscurations)
5. being purified of obstructive obscurations (i.e., obscurations to omniscience)
6. being purified of inferior obscurations (i.e., self-cherishing)
7. knowledge
8. freedom

The Two Causes of Going for Refuge

There are two main causes of going for refuge to the Three Jewels—these are fear and faith. In the context of refuge, fear refers to a fear of cyclic existence with all its sufferings and difficulties in general, as well as to a fear of the sufferings of the lower realms in particular. Having fear and wishing to be separated from the problems of cyclic existence, we seek someone or something that can provide us protection, just as a frightened person with problems looks for help and protection from someone more powerful. Through understanding the qualities of the Buddha, Dharma, and Sangha Jewels we develop faith and confidence that they can free us from the sufferings of cyclic existence. Thus, with fear and faith as a cause, we go for refuge to the Three Jewels.

Causal and Resultant Refuge

There are two ways of going for refuge—going for causal refuge and going for resultant refuge. Going for refuge to the beings who have already become enlightened is going for causal refuge to the Buddha Jewel; going for refuge to our own resultant buddha, the buddha we will become, is resultant refuge. Going for refuge to the realizations of true paths and true cessation in others' mental continua is causal refuge in the Dharma Jewel; going for refuge to our own future realizations is resultant refuge. Going for refuge to the superiors who have already become sangha is causal refuge in the Sangha Jewel; going for refuge to the sangha, the superiors we ourselves will become, is resultant refuge. Wishing to attain enlightenment, we should go for refuge to our own future resultant Buddha, Dharma, and Sangha as this will generate more interest in the practice of going for refuge and consequently we will put more energy into it.

Buddha Nature

When reciting the verse of refuge we should be completely convinced that we can definitely eliminate all our obscurations and thereby attain buddhahood. The reason for this certainty is that according to the sutra teachings every sentient being has buddha nature, or buddha lineage, and, in a similar context, the tantra teachings speak of tantra of basis. The explanation, common to both sutra and tantra, is that these refer to the mind's emptiness of

17

inherent, or true, existence. On a deeper level, tantra of basis is explained to be the subtle mind and subtle wind that transform into a buddha's body and mind. Due to the presence of buddha nature each and every sentient being has the potential to become buddha. Therefore, if we put effort into purifying our negativities and accumulating positive energy, or merit, we can be absolutely certain that we ourselves can become a buddha.

Refuge Advice

Upon deciding to take the Three Jewels as our main objects of refuge, we should abandon some actions and adopt others. In relation to the Buddha Jewel we should not take inferior mundane beings as our final refuge and we should respect all images of the Buddha equally, irrespective of the quality of the statue, painting, or drawing. To put our refuge in the Dharma Jewel into practice we should avoid harming sentient beings by abandoning the ten non-virtuous actions and engaging in the ten virtuous actions. Also we should respect all texts and books containing Dharma teachings. To uphold our refuge in the Sangha Jewel we should avoid people who influence us in a detrimental way and we should respect even the robes of the ordained. In addition to following the specific advice given in relation to each of the Three Jewels individually, we should also mentally recite one of the refuge prayers three times during the day and three times at night while remembering the qualities of the Buddha, Dharma, and Sangha. In this way we will continually develop and deepen our refuge in the Three Jewels.

II) The Mind of Enlightenment

Although the force of the basis includes both going for refuge and generating the mind of enlightenment, the generation of the mind of enlightenment is not explained in the commentary. However, it is an essential part of the practice of confession since negative actions committed in relation to sentient beings are purified by generating the mind that wishes to lead them to the perfect happiness of complete enlightenment.

We know of two methods to develop the mind of enlightenment, 1) the meditation on the seven, the six causes and one effect, and 2) the meditation on exchanging self and others. Since we will not be able to develop the mind of enlightenment as long as we continue to hold on to our biased attitudes toward sentient beings, each of these meditations is necessarily preceded by the preliminary practice of developing an attitude of equanimity toward all sentient beings.

1) The Seven: The Six Causes and One Effect

THE PRELIMINARY PRACTICE: MEDITATION ON EQUANIMITY

When developing the mind of enlightenment through meditating on the seven—six causes and one effect—the equanimity meditation is performed in relation to our friends, enemies, and strangers. The purpose of training in equanimity toward these three categories of people is to abandon the habit of generating hatred toward enemies, attachment toward friends, and indifference toward strangers. Through familiarizing ourselves with this meditation we will gradually stop making this distinction and learn to see all sentient beings as equal. This type of equanimity is common to both the Lesser Vehicle (*hīnayāna, theg dman*) and Great Vehicle (*mahāyāna, theg pa chen po*) traditions of Buddhism.

Begin the meditation by visualizing an enemy, a friend, and a stranger as if they were present in front of yourself. Having done so examine how you feel in regard to each of these people. You will probably find that toward the enemy you have a sense of aversion and repulsiveness; toward the friend warmth and attraction; and toward the stranger no emotion whatsoever. Then ask yourself, "What are the reasons I make these distinctions of enemy, friend, and stranger?" You will discover that you think of one person as your enemy because he or she has harmed you or your loved ones in the past, is presently harming you or your loved ones, or will harm you or your loved ones in the future. The reason you consider someone else a friend is that he or she has helped you or your loved ones in the past, is helping you or your loved ones in the present, or will help you or your loved ones in the future. You regard another person as a stranger because he or she has neither helped nor harmed you or your loved ones. As a result of these experiences you respectively feel hatred, attachment, and indifference toward these people. By analyzing this situation with wisdom we will come to the conclusion that we do not have valid reasons for making these distinctions since our perception of friends, enemies, and strangers is not at all stable. In fact, our relationships are constantly changing. Today's dearest friend can become tomorrow's enemy, today's worst enemy can become an intimate friend tomorrow, and someone now a stranger may eventually become a beloved friend or a hated enemy. From the level of our personal relationships up to the level of relationships between nations there is constant change.

Both in this life and throughout our beginningless succession of lives we have had many different relationships with each sentient being and in our future lives we will continue to have many different relationships with them. In addition to having had these three types of relationship with every sentient being, each one has also been our mother and has cared for us with infinite kindness and, even when they were not our mother, they helped and benefited us. Therefore, there is no reason to hate some sentient beings, to be attached to others, and to be indifferent toward still others.

These disturbing emotions bring us endless problems. For example, the pain of being abandoned by a friend is mainly due to our attachment. This attachment in turn can give rise to anger as a result of, for example, the jealousy we feel upon seeing our friend talking and laughing with another person. Since these and many other problems arise from attachment we should continually try to diminish and eventually eliminate it altogether. Reflecting on this we must make a firm decision that from now on we will not generate these harmful emotions toward other people.

THE ACTUAL MEDITATION ON THE SEVEN POINTS

Based on the development of equanimity we engage in the actual seven-point meditation composed of six causes and one effect. The first cause is the understanding that each and every sentient being has been our mother at some time during our beginningless lives in cyclic existence. Upon developing this understanding we go on to contemplate the second cause, remembering the kindness that we have received from our present mother (or another primary caretaker) that is then extrapolated to include all sentient beings. Thirdly, based on a deep sense of gratitude for the kindness we have received, we generate the wish to return this kindness. This in turn leads to the development of the fourth and fifth causes, love and compassion; respectively, the thought that wishes each sentient being happiness and the thought that wishes them to be free from suffering. As a consequence of developing love and compassion we develop the sixth cause, the special, or altruistic, attitude that is the decision to take upon ourselves the personal responsibility to bring all sentient beings happiness and freedom from suffering. Upon considering how to accomplish this we reach the conclusion that the only effective method is to achieve our own enlightenment. Thus, the effect, or outcome, of the previous six causes is the seventh point, the generation of the mind of enlightenment.[13]

2) EXCHANGING SELF AND OTHERS

The Preliminary Practice, Meditation on Equanimity

The second technique for developing the mind of enlightenment is the meditation on exchanging self and others, or more precisely, exchanging the attitude of cherishing ourselves for the attitude of cherishing others. The preliminary equanimity meditation associated with this practice is superior to, and more profound than, that of the equanimity meditation related to the seven causes and effect meditation. This is because the equanimity of the seven causes and effect meditation merely entails equalizing our attitude toward sentient beings while, in the context of exchanging self and others, equanimity is the strong intention to equally benefit and help all sentient beings without any partiality whatsoever. This type of equanimity eliminates the thought, "I will benefit this sentient being but not that sentient being." To develop this attitude it is necessary to depend on logical reasons, which are divided into (1) reasons based on the conventional truth and (2) reasons based on the ultimate truth.

(1) Reasons Based on the Conventional Truth

(a) Three reasons from the viewpoint of others
(i) We do not want to experience the slightest problem even in a dream and we are not satisfied even when we enjoy the greatest happiness. Likewise, even tiny sentient beings such as ants want only to experience happiness and do not want to experience even the smallest suffering. Since we are all equal in wanting happiness and not wanting suffering it is not right to be attached to our friends and to want to help them, and to hate our enemies and want to harm them. We should wish to benefit all sentient beings equally.

(ii) When we give food to a group of beggars, it would not be right to give food to some and not to others since all are equal in their hunger and need for food. Similarly, ourselves and all other ordinary sentient beings completely lack uncontaminated happiness and do not even experience perfect contaminated happiness. Since we are all equal in lacking happiness, although constantly wishing to obtain it, it would not be right to have the thought wishing to give happiness to some and not to others. We should wish to benefit all sentient beings equally.

(iii) In a hospital where there are many sick and suffering patients, it would not be right to treat some people while neglecting others. Likewise, ourselves and all sentient beings are completely the same in that each one of us is ill due to the three mental poisons of attachment, hatred, and ignorance. In consequence, we wander in cyclic existence experiencing the three types of suffering: the suffering of suffering, the suffering of change, and pervasive compounding suffering. The suffering of suffering includes both physical and mental suffering; the suffering of change refers to an experience that originally appears to be happiness but eventually changes into suffering; and pervasive compounding suffering is our contaminated aggregates, the bases of our present suffering and the creators of our future suffering. Since all sentient beings are equal in not wanting suffering yet continually experiencing it, we should have the strong wish to benefit all of them equally without the bias of thinking to help some and to neglect others.

Having meditated on these points and understanding that all sentient beings are equal, we may still wonder, "Why should I take the responsibility upon myself to help them?" To answer this question we contemplate the following three reasons.

(b) Three reasons from the viewpoint of self
(i) Each one of us has been taking rebirth in cyclic existence since beginningless time and in each of these many lives we have been dependent on sentient beings. Each sentient being has been our mother, relative, and friend and has helped and looked after us. In addition, sentient beings have provided us with, and are providing us with, the three essentials for our daily happiness—food, clothes, and a good reputation. For example, the food we eat comes from the hard work of farmers and the flesh of animals, the clothes we wear come from the textile makers and the skins of animals, and the encouragement and support we need come from other people.

Without depending on others we would not have even these basic happinesses. In addition, luxuries such as the ability to travel quickly and comfortably are also due to the kindness of others, the scientists, engineers, and so on. Even from the point of view of Dharma, the development of all our inner qualities is dependent on sentient beings who serve as the objects of our love, compassion, patience, and so forth. Consequently, even the highest happinesses, liberation and enlightenment, are dependent on sentient beings. Since all sentient beings are equal in having been kind to us and in having benefited us, we should firmly decide not to abandon any sentient being and to help each one without the slightest partiality.

(ii) We might think that while sentient beings have benefited us they have also harmed us. In response to this doubt we should think that sentient beings have definitely benefited us more than they have harmed us. In this life and in past lives the amount of benefit we have received from other sentient beings far outweighs the amount of harm. Therefore, it would not be right to abandon some sentient beings, we should have the intention to equally benefit all.

(iii) Although the moment of our death is uncertain, we will definitely die. It is the same for all other sentient beings. Since we are all caught in the web of impermanence, there is no sense in being attached to some sentient beings and to hate others. For example, a group of criminals who are scheduled for execution tomorrow do not hold feelings of attachment or hatred for each other, since all are going to die simultaneously. Likewise, since we and all other sentient beings are definitely going to die, there is no sense in discriminating. We should decide not to abandon even one sentient being and to help each one in whatever way we can.

This completes the six reasons in relation to the conventional truth from the viewpoint of both self and others. The next three reasons are in relation to the ultimate truth.

(2) Reasons Based on the Ultimate Truth

(i) Through mistaken conceptions we impute "friend" on the sentient beings who help us and "enemy" on those who harm us. If friend and enemy did in fact truly exist from their own side, rather than being mere imputations, Shākyamuni Buddha would have realized it. However, the Buddha made no distinction between a person who was applying oils and perfumes to one side of his body and another who was cutting the flesh of the other side. Therefore, since enemy and friend are just imputed by our own thought and do not exist from their own side we should decide to benefit all sentient beings equally.

(ii) In addition, if the enemy were truly existent he or she would always be an enemy and the truly existent friend would always be a friend. However, the reality is that our relationships, as well as our social status, wealth, and so on, are far from being stable. In fact they change frequently because there is no certainty at all in cyclic existence. Even this precious human rebirth is not stable—eventually we will die, take rebirth, and once again die. Therefore, we should abandon our concrete ideas concerning friends and enemies and resolve to benefit all sentient beings equally.

(iii) Self and others are dependent upon each other. For example, I refer to myself as "I" and to another person as "you," while that person would say "you" when referring to me and "I" when referring to himself or herself. I and you are established in dependence on each other and are not established independently from their own side. In the same way, tall and short, here and there, up and down, father and son, etc., only exist in relation to each other. A single person can be both father and son in dependence, respectively, on his relation to his son and his relation to his father. If these were not imputed by thought and established relatively, but instead existed inherently, then a father would always be a father and could never be a son. Likewise, enemy and friend are not truly existent but established in dependence. Therefore, there is no reason to be attached to the friend and to hate the enemy. Instead, we should wish to help all sentient beings equally.

THE ACTUAL MEDITATION ON EXCHANGING SELF AND OTHERS

Through relying on these nine reasons, we can equalize our attitude toward self and others and develop the wish to benefit all sentient beings equally. Having cultivated this equanimity we then strive to generate the mind of enlightenment by contemplating the following five points, each of which leads to a particular decision related to a verse from *The Offering to the Guru* (*Guru Puja, Lama Chöpa*).

(1) The Decision to Benefit All Sentient Beings Equally

Having contemplated the nine reasons based on the conventional and ultimate truths, we can see that there is no reason to develop attachment for friends, feeling them to be close, and hatred for enemies, feeling them to be distant. The afflictions that are most harmful to us in this and future lives are attachment and hatred. They are the causes of hundreds of sufferings. They are like a prison guard preventing us from leaving the prison of cyclic existence. They lead us to rebirth in hell. Even the unhappiness and suffering we experience in a dream are caused by attachment and hatred. Like a tumor growing within our body they continually cause us pain and suffering. Therefore, just as we would attempt to free ourselves of a tumor by seeking medical treatment, we should strive to eliminate attachment and hatred from our mental continuum.

The thought to benefit all sentient beings and to separate them from suffering is the best tool to obtain the goal of temporal and ultimate happiness for ourselves and others. Since the profound practice of all bodhisattvas is to cultivate the attitude wishing to benefit sentient beings, all the buddhas of the past, present, and future have traveled this path. Therefore, we too should develop the thought, "Whatever sentient beings from their side do to me it does not matter. Whether they help me or harm me is of no importance. From my side I will try to generate good thoughts toward them. I will help and benefit them in any way I can." Thinking like this, decide to develop the thought to benefit all sentient beings equally and request your guru, who is inseparable from the deity, to bless you to develop this kind of attitude by reciting the following verse from *The Offering to the Guru:*

> Never desiring the slightest suffering,
> Never satisfied with the happiness we have,
> There is no difference between myself and others;
> Please bless me to generate joy in others' happiness.

While reciting this verse, contemplate its meaning and firmly decide to benefit and help all sentient beings without any partiality whatsoever.

(2) The Decision to Abandon Self-Cherishing

Having equalized self and others, we should now begin the meditation on exchanging self and others (i.e., exchanging self-cherishing for cherishing others). To do this it is necessary to first contemplate the numerous disadvantages of cherishing ourselves. For example, self-cherishing is the cause of all suffering, from the problems of human beings up to rebirth in hell. Self-cherishing is the reason why the foe-destroyers of the Lesser Vehicle fall into the extreme of nirvana.[14] Although they are liberated from cyclic existence, they remain in equipoise in a state of peace due to thinking of themselves more than others. Also some bodhisattvas take an especially long time to reach enlightenment, in spite of having generated the mind of enlightenment, because they still have some remaining traces of self-cherishing.

In short, all the defects of cyclic existence and beyond cyclic existence (liberation) are caused by self-cherishing. In our present life and in all our future lives the suffering that we will experience is caused by our attitude of cherishing ourselves more than others. Self-cherishing is like a poisonous seed that, when not destroyed, prevents the attainment of happiness and enlightenment. Therefore, we need to make the firm decision, "I will not generate the self-cherishing thought even for an instant," and then request the guru and the deity for blessings to be able to carry out this practice with the following verse from *The Offering to the Guru:*

> Having seen this chronic disease of self-cherishing
> As the cause producing unwanted suffering,
> Please bless me to blame, begrudge, and
> Destroy the great demon of selfishness.

Contemplate this verse and firmly decide to abandon self-cherishing. Although we may be afraid of the external demons who sometimes cause us illness and disease, in actuality the inner demon of self-cherishing is much more dangerous because it is the source of all our problems and suffering. When we experience problems, instead of pointing out the cause as other peoples' faults and mistakes, we should point to our own self-cherishing as the one to blame. Other sentient beings are, in fact, the source of all our happiness and good qualities.

If we were to fight with ordinary external enemies and then decide to give the victory to them, the problem would be solved and the conflict finished. However, we should never give the victory to our inner enemy, our self-cherishing. Instead, we should continually fight to conquer this enemy completely. Geshe Langri Tangpa in his *Eight Verses on Mind Training* (*bLo sbyong tsig rkang brgyad ma lo rgyus dang bcad pa*) said, "I will take the losses and defeats upon myself and I will give the victories and gains to others." By developing this attitude we will eventually achieve the stable, uncontaminated, everlasting happiness of the state of buddhahood and thereby possess the capacity to spontaneously and effortlessly fulfill the benefit of all sentient beings.

(3) The Decision to Cherish Others

Following upon the decision to abandon self-cherishing we need to contemplate the advantages of cherishing others. For example, whatever qualities, happiness, and good reputation we possess, all are the result of having cherished others. The happiness of humans and gods up to the bliss of buddhahood are the results of cherishing others.

Also, in terms of our Dharma practice, whether at the time of the base, path, or result, sentient beings are absolutely essential to us. At the time of the base (prior to entering the path of accumulation) we need sentient beings as referent objects toward whom we can develop compassion. At the time of the path, when practicing the six perfections, we need sentient beings as objects of our practice; for example, to practice generosity we need someone to accept our offerings. At the time of the result, the attainment of enlightenment, we also need sentient beings since a buddha turns the wheel of Dharma (i.e., teaches) only for their benefit. Therefore, sentient beings are absolutely essential to us at the beginning, middle, and end of our practice.

Having contemplated the advantages of cherishing others the third decision is, "From the side of sentient beings whether they harm me or benefit me it does not matter. I will hold them all as equal. I will cherish all sentient beings as I cherish my guru and my deity. I will not abandon any sentient being but will always cherish each of them. I will not abandon the attitude of cherishing others even for an instant." Then request the guru and the deity to bless you to be able to do this by reciting this verse from *The Offering to the Guru:*

Having seen the mind that cherishes my mothers and
Would set them in bliss as the gateway to the arising of infinite
  qualities,
Even should these migrators arise as my enemies,
Please bless me to cherish them more than my life.

(4) The Decision to Exchange Self and Others

Having examined the disadvantages of self-cherishing and the advantages of cherishing others we should actually practice exchanging the thought that cherishes self for the thought that cherishes others. However, at this point we might experience some doubts concerning the difficulty of making this exchange and perhaps think that it is not actually possible to accomplish it. To eliminate this doubt we need to consider that in the past even Shākyamuni Buddha was an ordinary person just like ourselves. In fact, at times we were born together with him in cyclic existence. However, unlike ourselves, the Buddha put effort into the practice of exchanging self and others and thereby succeeded in attaining enlightenment. Instead, we, who have continued to cherish ourselves since beginningless time and have been concerned only with fulfilling our own aims, are still wandering in cyclic existence. Reflecting upon this we will realize that we too are indeed capable of exchanging ourselves with others, we just need to make the necessary effort. Through familiarity with the attitude of cherishing others, we can even arrive at the point of thinking of others' bodies as our own, just as now, due to familiarity, we cherish our body, although at one time it was merely the combination of our mother's egg and father's sperm and therefore belonged to them.

Understanding that it is possible to cherish others as we now cherish ourselves, we should make the decision, "Since I can exchange myself and others, I will do so right now," and then request the guru and the deity for blessings to be able to do so by reciting this verse from *The Offering to the Guru:*

In brief, the childish work only for their own welfare,
While the buddhas work solely for the welfare of others;
With a mind realizing the contrast between their respective faults and
  qualities,
Please bless me to be able to equalize and exchange myself and others.

(5) The Decision to Make Our Heart Practice the Exchanging of Self and Others

To reinforce the decision to exchange ourselves and others, we should alternately contemplate the disadvantages of self-cherishing and the advantages of cherishing others. Think, for example, that due to cherishing ourselves we engage in killing other sentient beings and thereby will experience the consequences of rebirth in hell and, later on when reborn again as a human being, a short life. Then think that through cherishing others and thereby refraining from killing, we will experience the happy results of rebirth in the higher realms and a long life as a human being. In this manner, alternately consider the suffering results of each of the ten non-virtuous actions and the benefits of engaging in the corresponding virtuous action. Having done so the conclusion reached is that all faults, misery, and unpleasantness are generated by self-cherishing while all qualities, benefits, and fortune come about through cherishing others. At this point we should make the decision to definitely exchange ourselves with others thinking, "No matter whom I encounter I will not abandon the practice of cherishing others. I will make my heart practice the exchanging of self with others." To be able to do so request the guru and the deity for blessings by reciting the following verse from *The Offering to the Guru:*

> Self-cherishing is the gateway to all misfortune,
> While cherishing my mothers is the foundation of every quality;
> Therefore, please bless me to make my heart practice
> The yoga of exchanging self and others.

Then, on the basis of having made the decision to cherish others, we engage in the actual practice of exchanging self and others by way of a meditation known as "taking and giving." Begin by visualizing your self-cherishing in the form of a heap of black dust at your heart. In front of yourself visualize all sentient beings who, due to having committed negative actions, are experiencing suffering and difficulties. Motivated by compassion, imagine taking their suffering from them in the form of thick black smoke that leaves their bodies through their right nostrils. This smoke enters into your own left nostril and, descending, strikes the self-cherishing at your heart exploding it into tiny pieces. Your self-cherishing completely disappears. Imagine that all sentient beings are freed from their suffering. Then, motivated by love, breathe out all your roots of virtue, possessions, and happiness of the past, present, and future through your right nostril in the form of white light. This light enters the sentient beings through their left nostrils giving them every desired happiness, from the mundane up to the supreme happiness of unsurpassed enlightenment.

Although by doing this meditation on "taking and giving" we cannot actually take away the suffering of sentient beings nor can we give them our happiness, we can increase our good heart while decreasing our self-cherishing and self-grasping. If we are able to do this practice daily, even for just a few minutes, it will definitely bring beneficial results. In addition, we can continue to develop our good heart throughout the day, whether walking, eating, sitting, or resting, by constantly thinking to benefit others and to avoid causing them harm. This good heart is the essence of cherishing others.

3

The Force of Applying All Antidotes

THE BENEFITS OF PROSTRATING TO THE THIRTY-FIVE TATHĀGATAS AND RECITING THEIR NAMES

I prostrate to [Teacher] Bhagavan Tathāgata Foe-Destroyer Perfectly
  Complete Buddha Glorious Conqueror Shākyamuni.
I prostrate to Tathāgata Thoroughly Destroying With Vajra Essence.
I prostrate to Tathāgata Radiant Jewel.
I prostrate to Tathāgata Nāga-Lord King.
I prostrate to Tathāgata Army of Heroes.
I prostrate to Tathāgata Delighted Hero.[15]
I prostrate to Tathāgata Jewel Fire.
I prostrate to Tathāgata Jewel Moonlight.
I prostrate to Tathāgata Meaningful to Behold.
I prostrate to Tathāgata Jewel Moon.
I prostrate to Tathāgata Immaculate.
I prostrate to Tathāgata Bestowed With Courage.[16]
I prostrate to Tathāgata Purity.
I prostrate to Tathāgata Bestowed With Purity.
I prostrate to Tathāgata Water-God.
I prostrate to Tathāgata Water-God Deity.
I prostrate to Tathāgata Glorious Excellence.
I prostrate to Tathāgata Glorious Sandalwood.
I prostrate to Tathāgata Infinite Splendor.
I prostrate to Tathāgata Glorious Light.
I prostrate to Tathāgata Glorious Sorrowless.
I prostrate to Tathāgata Son of Cravingless.
I prostrate to Tathāgata Glorious Flower.

I prostrate to Tathāgata Pure Light Rays Clearly Knowing by Sporting.
I prostrate to Tathāgata Lotus Light Rays Clearly Knowing by Sporting.
I prostrate to Tathāgata Glorious Wealth.
I prostrate to Tathāgata Glorious Mindfulness.
I prostrate to Tathāgata Glorious Name Widely Renowned.
I prostrate to Tathāgata Most Powerful Victory Banner King.
I prostrate to Tathāgata Glorious Utterly Suppressing.
I prostrate to Tathāgata Totally Victorious in Battle.
I prostrate to Tathāgata Glorious Suppressing Advancement.
I prostrate to Tathāgata Glorious All-Illuminating Manifestations.
I prostrate to Tathāgata Jewel Lotus Suppresser.
I prostrate to Tathāgata Foe-Destroyer Perfectly Complete Buddha
Mountain-Lord King Firmly Seated on Jewels and a Lotus.

When the benefits of prostrating to the thirty-five tathāgatas and reciting their names are explained from the outset, a strong interest will arise in the confession of negativities; therefore, I will mention them.

Reciting, "I prostrate to Tathāgata Shākyamuni," purifies the negativities of ten thousand eons. Similarly, Vajra Essence purifies the negativities of ten thousand eons; Radiant Jewel purifies the negativities of twenty thousand eons; Nāga-Lord King purifies the negativities of one thousand eons; Army of Heroes purifies the negativities of one thousand eons; Delighted Hero purifies the negativities of two thousand eons; Jewel Fire purifies the negativities of two thousand eons; Jewel Moonlight purifies the negativities of eight thousand eons; Meaningful to Behold purifies the negativities of one eon; Jewel Moon purifies the negativities of the five actions of immediate [retribution]; Immaculate purifies the negativities of the five secondary [actions]; Bestowed With Courage purifies the negativities motivated by hatred; Purity purifies the negativities motivated by attachment; Bestowed With Purity purifies the negativities of ten thousand eons; Water-God purifies the negativities of one thousand eons; Water-God Deity purifies the negativities of five thousand eons; Glorious Excellence purifies the negativities of five thousand eons; Glorious Sandalwood purifies the negativities of seven eons; Infinite Splendor purifies the negativities of seven eons; Glorious Light is said to be of immeasurable benefit; Glorious

Sorrowless purifies the negativities motivated by ignorance; Son of Cravingless purifies the negativities instigated by imprints; Glorious Flower purifies all obscurations of body; Pure Light Rays purifies all obscurations of speech; Lotus Light Rays purifies all obscurations of mind; Glorious Wealth purifies all obscurations of misusing the possessions of the sangha; Glorious Mindfulness purifies all obscurations of disparaging people; Glorious Name purifies all obscurations motivated by jealousy; Most Powerful Victory Banner purifies all obscurations motivated by pride; Utterly Suppressing eliminates all types of divisive speech; Totally Victorious in Battle eliminates all types of afflictions; Suppressing Advancement eliminates the negativities of having caused others to commit [negativities]; Glorious All-Illuminating Manifestations eliminates the obscurations of rejoicing in [negativities] committed by others; Jewel Lotus eliminates the obscurations of having abandoned the Dharma; and Mountain-Lord King eliminates the obscurations of having degenerated our commitments to the guru.

It is said in the sutra that reciting or remembering the names of these tathāgatas one time purifies the negativities of countless eons. Keeping these benefits in mind you should put effort into confession.

Merely reciting the names of the thirty-five tathāgatas purifies the many negativities, even very heavy ones, that have been accumulated over a period of eons. Indeed, saying the mantra of Shākyamuni Buddha, "Tayathā Oṃ Muni Muni Mahāmunaye Shākyamunaye Svāhā," is equivalent to saying, "I prostrate to Teacher Bhagavan Tathāgata Foe-Destroyer Perfectly Complete Buddha Glorious Conqueror Shākyamuni." As it says in the commentary, merely reciting Shākyamuni Buddha's name purifies the negativities accumulated over a period of ten thousand eons. Therefore, when we are either too tired or too busy to recite the names of each of the thirty-five buddhas to purify whatever negativities we may have committed during the day, it is enough to merely recite Shākyamuni Buddha's name.

A Brief Explanation of the Negativities

The five actions of immediate retribution (*ānantarya, mtshams med*),[17] discussed in more detail below (see pp. 51–52), are, in brief, (1) killing your mother, (2) killing your father, (3) killing a foe-destroyer, (4) causing blood to flow from the body of a tathāgata with evil intent, and (5) creating a schism in the sangha. According to Vasubandhu's *Explanation of the 'Treasury of Knowledge'* the result of any of the first four actions is rebirth in the immediately subsequent life in one of the hell realms, while the result of creating a schism in the sangha is to definitely be reborn in the hell of greatest suffering, Unrelenting Torment (*avīchi, mnar med*).

The five secondary, or close, actions of immediate retribution (*upā-nantarīya, nye pa'i mtshams med*) are similar to the five actions of immediate retribution although they are somewhat less grave. The five are (1) killing a bodhisattva abiding in certainty (i.e., one who is certain to achieve buddha-hood within one hundred eons); (2) killing a superior; (3) destroying a stupa, monastery, temple, etc. with hatred; (4) raping a fully ordained nun who is a foe-destroyer; and (5) appropriating the provisions of the sangha (i.e., stealing statues or the sangha's belongings). Like the five actions of immediate retribution the five secondary also bring rebirth in hell in the immediately subsequent life.

The negativities committed due to the motivating force of the three poisonous minds, attachment, hatred, and ignorance, include the ten non-virtuous paths of actions, which consist of the three of body (killing, stealing, and sexual misconduct), the four of speech (lying, divisive speech, harsh words, and idle talk), and the three of mind (covetousness, malice, and wrong view).

There are two explanations of the meaning of obscurations of body (*lus kyi sgrib pa*). In some contexts, obscurations of body are explained to mean that the bodies of some sentient beings, such as those of animals, are obscured in the sense that when a being is born with that type of body the mind is obscured. Several stories from the vinaya teachings illustrate this. One tells of a fully ordained monk who, having achieved the power of magical emanation, transformed himself into a tiger. As a result his mind became completely obscured and he was no longer able to remember that he was actually a human being and a monk. This particular type of obscuration of body is also known as a maturation obscuration (*vipāka-āvaraṇa, rnam smin gyi sgrib pa*). Although at the moment we have clear minds and are intelligent, if we were to take rebirth as, for example, a sheep, our minds would become completely obscured by ignorance; consequently, we would become extremely foolish. While the mind of that sheep would be the continuity of our present mind, the change in body causes the mind to become obscured.

Obscurations of body can also refer to the obscurations, or negativities, accumulated by the three non-virtuous paths of action of the body. Therefore, purifying the obscurations of body includes purification of the causes for being reborn with an obscured mind due to an inferior body, as well as purification of the negativities created through actions of the body.

Obscurations of speech (*ngag gi sgrib pa*) are the negativities accumulated by the four non-virtuous paths of action of speech.

Obscurations of mind (*yid kyi sgrib pa*) are the negativities accumulated by the three non-virtuous paths of action of the mind as well as the afflictions that obscure, or cover, the mind.

Obscurations of misusing the possessions of the sangha refer to negativities accumulated through using the belongings of the sangha without permission, damaging them, or even throwing them away. Since these objects should be taken care of and treated with respect, misusing them is very negative and causes our minds to become obscured.

Obscurations of disparaging people, whether individuals or the sangha as a group, are the negativities of verbally belittling others by saying that they do not have qualities that they do in fact possess.

Obscurations motivated by jealousy refer to negativities committed out of jealousy, a mental factor that cannot bear the happiness of others. It derives from the root affliction, anger, and is the cause of many negative actions.

Obscurations motivated by pride refer to negativites committed due to pride. Pride is a huge obstacle to gaining new knowledge as it either causes us to think we know something that we do not know, or else it prevents us from admitting that we do not know something that we do not. In different contexts pride is divided into three, seven, or nine types, the worst type being the pride that is similar to the view of the transitory collection, that of a very strong sense of I. This sense of I, and its consequent sense of mine, are the causes of many obscurations.

Divisive speech means to purposely speak in such a way as to create a division between people, whether bringing about a rift between those who were harmonious or bringing about a greater rift between those who were already in discord.

All types of afflictions include the six root afflictions (attachment, anger, pride, ignorance, doubt, and afflicted view) and twenty secondary afflictions (belligerence, resentment, concealment, spite, jealousy, miserliness, deceit, dissimulation, haughtiness, harmfulness, non-shame, non-embarrassment, lethargy, excitement, non-faith, laziness, non-conscientiousness, forgetfulness, non-introspection, distraction),[18] the causes of all our negativities.

The negativities of making others commit negativities are created by ordering, asking, or paying someone else to engage in a negative action, such as murder. Even though we did not do the action directly ourselves, if it is carried out successfully, it is a complete action of killing and therefore brings the same results as if we had in fact actually committed it.

Obscurations of rejoicing in negativities done by others refer to the negativities we create through rejoicing that someone else has committed a negative action; for example, being happy and thinking that a hunter has done something good by successfully shooting and killing an animal.

Abandoning the Dharma, said to be the heaviest of all negative actions, causes the mind to become very obscured. *The Guhyasamāja Tantra* mentions that although the five actions of immediate retribution can be purified by the practice and recitation of that tantra, it cannot purify the negative action of having abandoned the holy Dharma. We commit the action of abandoning the Dharma by, for example, putting Dharma texts under inferior objects or by sitting on them. We also abandon the Dharma through criticizing our own or other religions. Practicing a religion for some time and later coming to feel uncomfortable with it and, as a result, deciding to stop practicing it for a while, is not the negative action of abandoning the Dharma. However, if we were to think that the religion is mistaken, has no result, and consequently completely reject it, the action would be that of abandoning the Dharma.

Obscurations of having degenerated our commitments to the guru occur by, for example, verbally criticizing or physically striking him or her.

In conclusion, reciting or remembering the names of the thirty-five tathāgatas purifies the many types of negativities that we have committed in this and previous lives. By understanding and reflecting on these benefits, even if we recite the names of the tathāgatas just once, we will purify the negativities accumulated over many eons.

THE VISUALIZATION

When doing the confession, visualize in the space in front of yourself the conqueror Shākyamuni in the middle, with the other tathāgatas in the four directions, above, and below, [each of whom is] seated on a moon cushion, a lotus, and a throne ornamented with jewels. Then, with your body prostrate; with your speech recite the names of the tathāgatas; and with your mind devoutly pay homage by remembering the benefits of prostrations and the qualities of the tathāgatas.

When doing the confession in the presence of the thirty-five tathāgatas visualize Shākyamuni Buddha seated on a large throne in front of yourself at the level of your eyebrows. He is surrounded in space by the other thirty-four buddhas, each of whom also has one face, two arms, wears the three robes of a fully ordained monk, and is seated on a moon cushion, lotus, and throne. Imagine that they are all actually present and, if possible, clearly visualize the specific colors and hand positions of each buddha. If you are unable to do this extensive visualization, merely visualize Shākyamuni Buddha seated on a moon cushion, lotus, and large throne and feel that the other tathāgatas are also present.

Then, with a clear visualization, whether detailed or simple, begin the confession by reciting the verse of going for refuge to the Three Jewels while simultaneously generating the wish to attain enlightenment for the benefit of all sentient beings. Develop a deep sense of regret for the many negative actions you have committed since beginningless time up to now. Then make a firm resolution to at least try to refrain from engaging in them in the future. With these states of minds—refuge, the mind of enlightenment, regret, and resolve—perform the actual antidote, the recitation of the names of the tathāgatas together with prostrations. By performing the confession in this manner, all four opponent forces are present and, with faith in the efficacy of this practice, we will definitely purify our negativities.

の ✿ の

Colors and Hand Positions of the Thirty-five Tathāgatas

TATHĀGATA	COLOR	HAND POSITION
Shākyamuni	yellow	right pressing down the earth left meditative equipoise
Thoroughly Destroying With Vajra Essence	yellow	two hands expounding Dharma
Radiant Jewel	red	two hands meditative equipoise
Nāga-Lord King	blue below neck white above neck	two hands at the heart, thumbs aligned in the middle, two [index] fingers straight, the tips slightly apart, [other fingers intertwined and] curled inward
Army of Heroes	yellow	right granting refuge left slightly drawn aside from the heart, the thumb and palm facing outward
Delighted Hero	yellow	two hands expounding Dharma
Jewel Fire	red	right pressing down the earth left meditative equipoise
Jewel Moonlight	white	right pressing down the earth left meditative equipoise
Meaningful to Behold	green	right granting refuge left slightly drawn aside from the heart, the thumb and palm facing outward
Jewel Moon	white	[two hands] expounding Dharma
Immaculate	blue	[two hands] meditative equipoise
Bestowed With Courage	yellow	[two hands] expounding Dharma
Purity	yellow	right pressing down the earth left meditative equipoise
Bestowed With Purity	red	[two hands] expounding Dharma
Water-God	white	[two hands] meditative equipoise
Water-God Deity	white	[two hands] expounding Dharma
Glorious Excellence	yellow	right granting refuge left slightly drawn aside from the heart, the thumb and palm facing outward

Glorious Sandalwood	white	right pressing down the earth left meditative equipoise
Infinite Splendor	red	[two hands] expounding Dharma
Glorious Light	blue	[two hands] expounding Dharma
Glorious Sorrowless	pink	[two hands] meditative equipoise
Son of Cravingless	yellow	[two hands] expounding Dharma
Glorious Flower	yellow	right granting refuge left slightly drawn aside from the heart, the thumb and palm facing outward
Pure Light Rays	yellow	right pressing down the earth left meditative equipoise
Lotus Light Rays	red	right pressing down the earth left meditative equipoise
Glorious Wealth	blue	[two hands] meditative equipoise
Glorious Mindfulness	yellow	[two hands] meditative equipoise
Glorious Name Widely Renowned	white	right expounding Dharma left meditative equipoise
Most Powerful Victory Banner	blue	right hoists a victory banner in direction of left shoulder left meditative equipoise
Utterly Suppressing	blue	right holds a sword at the heart left meditative equipoise
Totally Victorious in Battle	blue	two hands hold a yellow coat of mail
Suppressing Advancement	blue	two hands pressing down the earth
All-Illuminating Manifestations	red	right granting refuge, left meditative equipoise
Jewel Lotus Suppresser	orange	right granting refuge left meditative equipoise
Mountain-Lord King	yellow	two hands meditative equipoise holding a mountain

OBJECTS OF PROSTRATION

If it is asked, "Well then, to which objects should we prostrate and how should we prostrate?" Among the prostrations to the thirty-five tathāgatas—the objects—how to prostrate to the conqueror Shākyamuni, who is situated in the middle, is shown at the beginning saying, "I prostrate to Bhagavan Tathāgata Foe-Destroyer Perfectly Complete Buddha Glorious Conqueror Shākyamuni."

If the meaning of these [epithets] are explained a little:

Since he has destroyed (*bcom*) the four demons (*māra, bdud*), is endowed with (*ldan*) the four bodies and five exalted wisdoms, and has transcended (*'das*) cyclic existence and nirvana, he is called Bhagavan (*bcom ldan 'das*, Transcendent Endowed Destroyer).

Since he knows that he has gone (*gshegs pa*) to the direct perception of all phenomena and the thusness (*de bzhin nyid*) of all phenomena, he is called Tathāgata (*de bzhin gshegs pa*, One Gone Thus).

Since he has destroyed (*bcom*) the foes (*dgra*), which are the afflictions, he is called Foe-Destroyer (*arhat, dgra bcom pa*).

Since he has completed (*rdzogs pa*) all qualities perfectly (*yang dag pa*), precisely as they should be, he is called Perfectly Complete (*samyaksaṁ, yang dag par rdzogs pa*).

Since he has awakened (*sangs*) from the sleep of the afflictions and has expanded (*rgyas*) his awareness to all objects of knowledge, he is called Buddha (*sangs rgyas*, Awakened-Expanded). It is said, "Due to having awakened from the sleep of the afflictions and having expanded his awareness to objects of knowledge, the Buddha, like a lotus, is awakened and expanded."

Since he is endowed with the perfection of high status (*abhyudaya, mngon mtho*) and definite goodness (*niḥshreyasa, nges legs*), he is called Glorious (*shrī, dpal*).

Since he has conquered (*rgyal*) all objects of abandonment, the discordant class, he is called Conqueror (*jina, rgyal ba*).

Since he was born in the Shākya lineage, he is called Shākya.

Since he has subdued (*thub*) the foes that are the afflictions, he is called Muni (*thub pa*, Subduer).

Ꮤ ❖ Ꮤ

'Bhagavan' is an epithet given to a fully enlightened buddha, such as Shākyamuni Buddha. The etymology explained here accords with the Tibetan translation as *Chom-den-de* (Transcendent Endowed Destroyer). *Chom*, destroyer, indicates that the Buddha has destroyed all four demons, or māras: (1) the demon of the aggregates, (2) the demon of the afflictions, (3) the demon of death, and (4) the demon of the sons-of-the-gods. The demon of the aggregates in this particular context specifically refers to our contaminated body. Our body is called a demon because it is the base of all our suffering and problems. The demon of the afflictions refers to the mental afflictions of attachment, anger, ignorance, and so forth. They are called demons because they destroy our present happiness and create our future suffering. Death is called a demon because it causes harm to our body and mind through ending their relationship. The demon of the sons-of-the-gods refers to actual beings of the highest level of the desire realm, that of Controlling Others' Emanations, who harm us by sending five arrows, or negative energies, that disturb our peace of mind. When we feel angry right from the moment of waking it is because we have been struck by the arrow of anger, a type of negative energy, sent by the sons-of-the-gods. On the other hand, if from the time of waking we feel very slow and stupid it is a result of having been struck by the arrow of ignorance. When we are overcome with strong attachment it is due to having been struck by the arrow of attachment; being filled with excessive pride is due to the arrow of pride; and being tormented by jealousy is due to the arrow of jealousy. Each of us has, at some time, definitely experienced the results of the negative, harmful energy sent by the sons-of-the-gods.

Shākyamuni Buddha and all other buddhas are called Destroyer because they have completely destroyed their own demons of the aggregates, afflictions, and death, as well as having destroyed the demon of the sons-of-the-gods in the sense that a buddha can no longer be harmed by them.

The *den* of *Chom-den-de* means "to be endowed with" or "to possess." Since the Buddha possesses the four bodies and five exalted wisdoms he is called Endowed. The four bodies are the nature body, wisdom body, enjoyment body, and emanation body of an enlightened being. The five exalted wisdoms are the mirror-like wisdom, the wisdom of equality, the wisdom of individual realization, the wisdom of accomplishing activities, and the wisdom of the sphere of phenomena.[19]

De means "transcended" or "gone beyond." The Buddha is called Transcendent because he has transcended both cyclic existence and the nirvana of the hearer and solitary realizer foe-destroyers. Cyclic existence is the joining with contaminated aggregates again and again (i.e., the uncontrolled taking of rebirth) by the power of contaminated actions and afflictions. Nirvana, explained simply, is the attainment of a personal peaceful state of continuous meditative equipoise. Unlike ordinary sentient beings who are trapped in cyclic existence and the Lesser Vehicle foe-destroyers who have merely achieved their own peace, a buddha has attained a state of enlightenment that is free from both the faults of cyclic existence and those of nirvana and has thus fulfilled both his own and others' welfare.

In summary, the title of Bhagavan signifies that a buddha such as Shākyamuni Buddha, has abandoned all faults and has attained all qualities and is therefore worthy of our prostrations.

The Buddha is also called Tathāgata, One Gone Thus, because he has gone to, or reached, the simultaneous direct perception of all phenomena together with their thusness (i.e., emptiness). A tathāgata is also known as a *sugata* (*bde bar gshegs pa*, One Gone to Bliss) of which there are two types, the actual sugata being the realization of uncontaminated exalted wisdom. In addition, the complete abandonment of all objects of abandonment, the afflictions and so on, is also called sugata. Since a buddha has developed these qualities of realization and abandonment in his mental continuum he is called a sugata.

Although in many contexts the title of foe-destroyer refers specifically to the hearers and solitary realizers who have achieved their own personal liberation, it is also an epithet of the Buddha, since a foe-destroyer (*dgra bcom pa*) is a being who has completely destroyed (*bcom*) the inner foes, or enemies (*dgra*), the afflictions. The afflictions are called enemies because they harm us, just as do our external enemies. Recognizing that all our past, present, and future suffering is caused by our real enemies, the afflictions, we should continually strive to weaken them and finally destroy them altogether. In this way, we too will become foe-destroyers.

The Buddha is said to be Perfectly Complete since he has achieved the perfect completion of all qualities of body, speech, and mind. These qualities can be summarized, respectively, as the one hundred and twelve major and minor marks that adorn a buddha's body, the sixty-four qualities of a buddha's melodious speech, and the twenty-one divisions of uncontaminated exalted wisdom of a buddha's mind.

The Buddha is Glorious in that he possesses the perfection of high status, rebirth in the upper realms as a human, and the perfection of definite goodness, the state of omniscience that is endowed with qualities common to the hearers and solitary realizer foe-destroyers, and with qualities unique only to a buddha.

The Buddha is called Conqueror since he has conquered, or destroyed, the objects of abandonment, the afflictive obscurations that prevent liberation, and the obscurations to omniscience, or the obscurations to objects of knowledge, that prevent enlightenment. In other contexts, the epithet of Conqueror is explained to mean that a buddha has conquered the four demons.

The Buddha is known as Shākya since Shākya is the name of his family lineage or clan. The title of Muni, Subduer, demonstrates that the Buddha has subdued, or defeated, all the afflictions.

Although each one of us was born together with Shākyamuni Buddha many times in the past and we wandered with him in cyclic existence, the difference between the Buddha and ourselves is that in his previous lives he made an effort to complete the two collections of merit and wisdom and was thereby able to attain the state of enlightenment. We too, through making an effort, can attain high status, rebirth as a human or god in our future lives, or achieve the state of definite goodness, liberation and enlightenment. However, as long as we do not make the necessary effort, we will continue wandering in cyclic existence. Therefore, in this very life we need to make effort—not to make money, money, money—but to purify our minds so that we ourselves can become holy beings.

How to Prostrate

How to prostrate to him, the Subduer, who was described so, is as taught in *The Sutra of the Prayer of Good Conduct* (*Ārya bhadra-charyāpraṇidhānarāja*, *'Phags pa bzang po spyod pa'i smon lam gyi rgyal po*):

Emanate bodies equaling the number of atoms in the world systems, then prostrate touching your five body parts to the ground while visualizing that the emanated bodies also prostrate touching their five body parts to the ground. Emanate countless heads on your own body and on each of the emanated bodies and countless tongues in each head, then with your speech recite the ocean-like qualities of the objects of prostration, whichever of the thirty-five tathāgatas and so on. With your mind visualize the buddhas together with their children, who, equaling the number of grains of sand of the Ganges River, are seated on top of a single atom. Then, in brief, visualizing the entire earth and space filled with the buddhas together with their retinues of bodhisattvas, pay homage to them out of respect.

Likewise, the remaining root text (*grantha, gzhung*),[20] "I prostrate to Tathāgata Thoroughly Destroying With Vajra Essence" and so on, should also be understood in terms of this method of explaining by means of the two [divisions]: (1) to which objects to prostrate and (2) how to prostrate.

To perform actual physical prostrations (see appendix 7) begin by joining the palms of your hands with the thumbs folded inward. This represents offering a wish-fulfilling jewel to all the buddhas and surrounding bodhisattvas who are visualized in the space in front of yourself. Imagine emanating countless bodies each of which has many heads with many tongues and then touch your folded hands to four points in succession (crown, forehead, throat, and heart) or, if you prefer, to just three (crown, throat, and heart). As you prostrate, touch your five body parts (legs, arms, and head) to the ground and imagine that all the emanated bodies do the same. Simultaneously recite the name of the corresponding tathāgata while imagining that each of the emanated tongues also does the same. Since even doing a single prostration brings the result of taking rebirth as a universal monarch, we collect innumerable virtues by conjoining prostrations and recitation of the names of the tathāgatas with this visualization because, by doing so, it is equivalent to performing countless prostrations and recitations simultaneously.

OFFERINGS

The root text, [I prostrate to Tathāgata...], shows both the limb of prostration and the limb of offering since, having explicitly shown prostrations to the thirty-five buddhas, it also implicitly shows the necessity of making offerings.

In addition to prostrating to the thirty-five buddhas, we should also present various types of offerings to them. Outer offerings are either actual material substances such as the seven usually placed on an altar (drinking water, washing water, flowers, incense, light, perfume, and food) or mentally emanated offerings such as beautiful gardens, flowers, mountains, trees, lakes, and so on. In brief, all the enjoyable things that exist in this world can be mentally offered to the buddhas. In addition, we can offer our Dharma practice, our virtuous actions, just as the Tibetan saint Milarepa, who had no material offerings, offered his teacher, Marpa, his Dharma practice and realizations to repay the kindness he had received from him. In the context of tantra we offer even the objects of our attachment, hatred, and ignorance by including them in the *maṇḍala* offering, a representation of the universe that is purified and offered. By doing so we train ourselves to mentally offer the various objects that we, for example, presently hold so dear, just as Shākyamuni Buddha in his previous lives gave away everything he possessed, even his wife and child. Through making this type of offering the strength of our afflictions will gradually diminish.

4

The Force of Total Repudiation

REQUEST THE BUDDHA-BHAGAVANS TO WITNESS THE CONFESSION OF
NEGATIVITIES AND DOWNFALLS

*These and others, as many tathāgata foe-destroyer perfectly complete bud-
dha-bhagavans as are abiding, living, and residing in all the world systems
of the ten directions, all buddha-bhagavans, please pay attention to me.*

"These and others" indicates the thirty-five buddhas who were
explained above. "As many buddha-bhagavans as are abiding...in all
the world systems of the ten directions" indicates that they have
attained the truth body. "Living and residing" indicates that they have
attained the complete enjoyment body. "All buddha-bhagavans,
[please pay attention] to me" indicates that they have attained the
emanation body.

Saying, "Please pay attention to me," we request the thirty-five tathāgatas
and all the other buddhas of the ten directions to listen to, or to witness,
our confession. Since the buddhas who have attained the three bodies—the
truth body, enjoyment body, and emanation body—completely know all
that there is to know, they are therefore appropriate persons to whom to
make our confession.

The truth body encompasses the special mental qualities of a buddha, such
as the five exalted wisdoms. The enjoyment body, according to sutra, possesses the five qualities of (1) giving only Great Vehicle teachings, (2) being
surrounded solely by bodhisattva superiors, (3) being adorned with the
thirty-two major marks and eighty minor marks, (4) remaining until the
end of cyclic existence, and (5) always dwelling in the Not Low pure land

(*akaniṣṭa, 'og min*), so-called because it is the highest of the seventeen levels of the form realm. For the purpose of benefiting ordinary sentient beings who are unable to perceive it directly the enjoyment body emanates many bodies, the emanation bodies, to different realms and places in accordance with their needs.

> Having requested such buddha-bhagavans, those who have achieved the three bodies, to pay close attention to us with great mercy saying, "Please witness my confession of negativities and downfalls," it is necessary to put effort, day and night, into the confession of negativities and downfalls because it is taught in *The Heap of Jewels,* "Bodhisattvas, downfalls that are together with the five [actions of] immediate [retribution], downfalls that occur through women, downfalls that occur through the hands, downfalls that occur through children, downfalls that occur through stupas, downfalls that occur through the sangha, and heavy downfalls other than those should be confessed day and night by yourself alone in the presence of the thirty-five buddhas."

The five actions of immediate retribution, as mentioned previously, are killing one's mother, one's father, or a foe-destroyer, causing blood to flow from the body of a tathāgata with evil intent, and creating a schism in the sangha. A downfall that occurs through women transpires when, for example, a man with the lay vow of refraining from sexual misconduct has sexual intercourse with another man's wife. Downfalls that occur through the hands are, for example, killing and stealing, both of which are generally accomplished with our hands. Downfalls that occur through children include such actions as abusing a child, abandoning a newborn baby, and fighting over a child. Downfalls that occur through stupas encompass such actions as destroying stupas, taking the offerings made to them, taking their decorations, and so forth. Downfalls that occur through the sangha can be committed in relation to either the conventional sangha, a group of four fully ordained monks or nuns, or the ultimate sangha, a single superior. Examples of this type of downfall are stealing the belongings of the conventional or ultimate sangha or creating a schism in the conventional sangha.

These and other heavy downfalls need to be confessed day and night in front of the tathāgatas by applying the four opponent forces. In brief, as explained above, go for refuge from the depths of your heart to the Three Jewels while generating the wish to attain enlightenment to benefit all sentient beings, thereby completing the force of the basis. Then develop deep regret for the negative actions you have done and resolve to try not to do them again, thereby completing, respectively, the opponent force of total repudiation and that of turning away from faults in the future. With these three opponent forces as the foundation, prostrate while reciting the names of the tathāgatas, thereby completing the force of applying all antidotes. By confessing in this manner you will definitely be able to purify the negativities committed in this and previous lives.

IDENTIFYING NEGATIVITIES AND OBSCURATIONS

In this life and in all the states of rebirth in which I have circled in cyclic existence throughout beginningless lives, whatever negative actions I have done, caused to be done, or rejoiced in the doing of...

Negative actions [include] those directly committed in this life, those indirectly committed through having made others do them, and those of having rejoiced in others' doing of them, as well as those not committed in this life but committed throughout beginningless lives up to this life while continuously circling in cyclic existence by the power of actions and afflictions. In brief, the negativities to be confessed are shown to be (1) the negative actions that we have directly committed, (2) those that we have indirectly committed through having caused them to be done, and (3) those of having rejoiced in others' doing of them, in all the states of rebirth in which we have circled.

Here the root text clearly shows that it is necessary to confess and purify both the negativities committed in this life as well as those committed in previous lives. Although we have probably done many negative actions in this life, most likely we have not engaged in every single type. However, since our previous rebirths are without beginning we have certainly committed them at some time in the past. Therefore, it is extremely important to include all the negativities of this life and all those of our previous lives in the confession, whether they were committed directly, indirectly, or by rejoicing.

The Negativities of Misusing the Possessions of the Jewels

Whatever possessions of stupas, possessions of the sangha, or possessions of the sangha of the ten directions I have appropriated, made to be appropriated, or rejoiced in the appropriation of...

In this context a stupa is the Buddha Jewel and the Dharma Jewel; their possessions are their offering substances. Using them without permission is considered to be appropriating the possessions of a stupa. Thus, we have directly appropriated the possessions of the Buddha and Dharma Jewels. In addition, if, without permission, we directly use the possessions of the sangha—the belongings of superior beings, the actual Sangha Jewel—it is appropriating the possessions of the Sangha Jewel. Thereby, [the root text] indicates that the negativities of misusing the possessions of all three Jewels are negativities to be confessed.

"The possessions of the sangha of the ten directions" are the belongings of the sangha, a group of four or more, who live in the infinite places, the communities of sangha of the ten directions. Directly using [their possessions] without permission is appropriating the possessions of the sangha of the ten directions. This is also called appropriating the provisions of the sangha.

Since these objects are very delicate and these situations easily happen to us, I implore you to be careful concerning this point.

All our negativities of having appropriated the possessions of the Three Jewels as was explained—whether directly, indirectly (having made others appropriate them), or of having rejoiced in others' appropriating of them—are negativities to be confessed.

In this context the Buddha and Dharma Jewels are referred to by the term "stupa." The Buddha Jewel includes all enlightened beings as well as representations of them such as statues, paintings, and pictures. If, without asking permission, we were to use the offerings that have been made to them, we would commit the action of appropriating the possessions of the Buddha Jewel. The Dharma Jewel is represented by texts containing the Buddha's teachings. If, without asking permission, we were to take and use offerings placed before them, our action would be that of appropriating the possessions of the Dharma Jewel.

Taking the belongings of superiors without asking permission is appropriating the possessions of the Sangha Jewel. Taking the belongings of, or offerings made to, the conventional sangha, including a monastery or nunnery, without asking permission, is appropriating the possessions of the sangha of the ten directions.

In summary, the negativities, or objects to be confessed, comprise any of the above-mentioned actions that we ourselves have directly committed, indirectly committed, or accumulated through having rejoiced in others' doing of them.

The Negativities of the Five Actions of Immediate Retribution

> *Whatever of the five actions of immediate [retribution] I have done, caused to be done, or rejoiced in the doing of...*

The five actions of immediate [retribution] are causing blood to flow from the body of a tathāgata with evil intent, creating a schism in the sangha, killing a foe-destroyer, killing one's father, and killing one's mother. The negativities of having directly committed these actions ourselves, of having indirectly committed them through having made others do them, and of having rejoiced in others' doing of them are also negativities that are objects to be confessed.

There is a reason for calling these five "actions of immediate [retribution]": because if we commit any one of them, if it is not confessed, it will cause us to be thrown into hell after we die without another rebirth in between.

There is some difference of opinion between the Lesser and Greater Vehicles concerning whether or not we can actually commit the action of immediate retribution of causing blood to flow from the body of a tathāgata. According to the vinaya teachings this action can only be committed in relation to the body of Shākyamuni Buddha; consequently, it would be impossible for us to commit it. However, the Great Vehicle asserts that this action can be committed in relation to any tathāgata and, therefore, it would indeed be possible for us to commit it. Regardless of this difference of opinion, it is unlikely that we have committed this action in this life; nor is it likely that we have killed our father, our mother, or a foe-destroyer. On the other hand, it is impossible for us to have committed the action of immediate retribution of creating a schism in the sangha. This is because this particular action of immediate retribution is specifically related to an event that occurred during the lifetime of Shākyamuni Buddha when Devadatta imposed five mandatory practices that resulted in controversy within the monastery. The five practices were (1) to not eat meat because it involves the killing of sentient beings, (2) to not eat salty food because it causes attachment, (3) to not drink milk because it harms the suckling calf, (4) to not wear cut and sewn clothes because it harms the weavers, and (5) to not stay in solitary places because it does not benefit other people. Fortunately, harmony was quickly restored by two of Buddha's disciples, Shāriputra and Maudgalyāyana. In consequence, their presence, as well as that of Shākyamuni Buddha himself, is necessary to commit the action of immediate retribution of creating a schism in the sangha. In this lifetime, if we were to cause a division among the sangha, while it would be a great negativity, it would not be an action of immediate retribution.

Furthermore, according to the root tantra of Guhyasamāja, abandoning the Dharma is equivalent to the action of immediate retribution of creating a schism in the sangha, and breaking or destroying a statue of the Buddha is equivalent to the action of immediate retribution of causing blood to flow from a tathāgata. Therefore, according to tantra, it is possible that we have committed all five actions of immediate retribution at some time in this or past lives. Although we may not have committed any of them in this life, since we do not know with certainty that we did not do them in other lives, we need to purify them. For this reason, the actions of immediate retribution that we have directly and indirectly committed and the negativities accumulated by having rejoiced in others' doing of them are indicated as negativities to be confessed.

The Negativities Included in the Ten Non-virtues

> *Whatever of the ten non-virtuous paths of action I have engaged in the adoption of, caused to be engaged in, or rejoiced in the engagement in...*

The negativities of adopting the ten non-virtuous paths of action taught as, "actions of body, three types," and so forth, are also negativities to be confessed, or negativities that are objects to be confessed, whether we have directly engaged in them, have caused others to engage in them (i.e., have made others do them), or have rejoiced in others engaging in (i.e., doing) them.

The ten non-virtuous paths of action are the three accumulated by the body (killing, stealing, and sexual misconduct), the four accumulated by speech (lying, divisive speech, harsh words, and idle talk), and the three accumulated by mind (covetousness, malice, and wrong view). Each of these paths of action must consist of four branches, or parts, to be complete. These are (1) the basis (*gzhi*), (2) thought (*bsam pa*), (3) execution (*sbyor ba*), and (4) completion (*mthar thug*). The branch of basis refers to the particular object at which an action is directed. The branch of thought is further divided into three: recognition, affliction, and motivation. Recognition, or discrimination, is the clear and unmistaken identification of the object. The affliction is any of the three mental poisons: attachment, hatred, or ignorance. The motivation is the wish to engage in the action. The execution, or preparation, includes all the actions engaged in prior to the completion of the path of action. The completion is when the actual path of action is accomplished. By carefully analyzing the ten non-virtuous paths of action in terms of their four branches we will come to understand exactly what each one of them entails.

Killing. Taking the life of a sentient being, even that of the tiniest insect, is the most serious of the negative actions of body. The *basis* is the continuum of another sentient being. The *recognition* is the correct identification of the sentient being we wish to kill. The *affliction* involved can be any of the three poisons; for example, killing for food is done out of attachment, killing out of aversion is due to hatred, and killing for enjoyment is caused by ignorance. The *motivation* is the wish to kill. The *execution* of the action can be done directly—using a weapon, poison, mantra power, and so forth—or indirectly by causing someone else to kill. The *completion* of the action is that the other sentient being dies first. Consequently, if two people were to mortally wound each other simultaneously, the person who dies first would not create the complete action of killing. Likewise, although suicide is a very heavy negative action, it is not the complete path of action of killing.

Stealing. Stealing is taking the wealth or possessions of others without them having been given. The *basis* is an object possessed by another being. The *recognition* is the clear unmistaken identification of the object we intend to take. The *affliction* can be any one of the three—attachment, hatred, or ignorance. The *motivation* is the wish to take an object that has not been given (i.e., to separate that object from the person to whom it belongs). The *execution* can be carried out directly—using either force, stealth, or deceit—or indirectly by causing someone else to steal. The *completion* is, after taking the object, to feel a sense of satisfaction thinking, "Now it is mine."

Sexual misconduct. Sexual misconduct occurs in relation to four types of *basis*: an unsuitable person, an unsuitable bodily part, an unsuitable time, and an unsuitable place. An unsuitable person is someone else's partner, a close relation, a minor, or someone with a vow of chastity. An unsuitable bodily part is, for example, the mouth or anus. An unsuitable time is daytime, during pregnancy, or when one of the partners has taken the eight Mahāyāna precepts, since these include refraining from all sexual activity for twenty-four hours. An unsuitable place is in front of our guru, parents, or images of the buddhas, near a stupa, or in a temple. The correct *recognition* of our partner is not necessary to complete the path of action of sexual misconduct. The *affliction* accompanying sexual misconduct is generally attachment but can be hatred (e.g., rape) or ignorance (e.g., thinking that sexual intercourse is a way to gain spiritual realizations). The *motivation* is the wish to engage in sexual activity. The *execution* is sexual activity with an unsuitable person, with an unsuitable bodily part, at an unsuitable time, or in an unsuitable place. The *completion* is experiencing the pleasure of orgasm.

Lying. The *basis* is a person who is capable of understanding our words. The *recognition* is knowing that we are altering our discrimination; for example, saying that we have seen someone whom we have not seen or saying that we have not seen someone whom we have seen. The *affliction* can be either attachment, hatred, or ignorance. The *motivation* is the wish to alter the truth. The *execution* can be done by speaking, by making a physical gesture, or by remaining silent. The *completion* is that the other person understands what we have communicated.

Divisive speech. The *basis* is two or more people who have either a harmonious or a disharmonious relationship. The *recognition* of these people should be unmistaken. The *affliction* can be any of the mental poisons. The *motivation* must be to cause discord between harmonious people or to cause further discord between those who are already in disharmony. The *execution* involves speaking true or false words with an end to causing discord; for example, speaking in such a way as to cause a complete breakup of an already strained relationship between two friends. The *completion* is that the other people understand what we have said.

Harsh words. The *basis* is another sentient being. The *recognition* of the person we wish to hurt with our words should be unmistaken. The *affliction* can be any of the three mental poisons. The *motivation* is the wish to cause harm with our words. The *execution* involves saying something true or untrue, in either a rude or polite way. The *completion* is that the other person understands our words.

Idle talk. The *basis* is something trivial or insignificant. The *recognition* of what we are saying should not be mistaken. The *affliction* can be any of the three mental poisons. The *motivation* is the wish to say the insignificant words. The *execution* is to speak without a good purpose; for example, teaching Dharma for the purpose of gaining money or fame, reading books that decrease our interest in Dharma, singing worldly songs, telling jokes, and habitually complaining. The *completion* is to finish speaking the insignificant words. Although this non-virtuous action is by nature light, it can become heavy by way of committing it frequently.

Covetousness. The *basis* is the possessions or qualities of another person. The *recognition* is the correct identification of the object we desire to possess. The main *affliction* is attachment. The *motivation* is the wish to possess the object. The *execution* is the thought process considering how to obtain the object. The *completion* is the decision to obtain the object.

Malice. The *basis* is another sentient being. The *recognition* of the sentient being we desire to harm must be unmistaken. The main *affliction* is hatred. The *motivation* is the wish to harm by striking, beating, and so on. The *execution* is the thought process planning to harm that sentient being. The *completion* is the decision to harm that sentient being.

Wrong view. The *basis* is a phenomenon that exists, such as past and future lives, the law of action and result, the Three Jewels, the four noble truths, and the two truths. The *recognition* is thinking that what we believe is completely correct when in fact it is incorrect. The main *affliction* is ignorance. The *motivation* is the wish to deny the existence of the object. The *execution* is undertaking the denial, of which there are four types: (1) denying that causes, virtue and non-virtue, exist; (2) denying that the four types of result exist; (3) denying that functions exist (including, [i] denying that parents are needed to produce a child, [ii] denying that a seed is needed to produce a plant, [iii] denying the existence of coming and going—i.e., past and future lives, and [iv] denying the existence of miraculous rebirth); and finally (4) denying the existence of foe-destroyers. The *completion* is deciding to actively deny the object; for example, deciding to tell other people that past and future lives do not exist.

According to the vinaya teachings, eight of the ten non-virtuous paths of action—sexual misconduct, the four of speech, and the three of mind—must be committed directly to become a complete action, while killing and stealing can be complete actions even when we cause someone else to do them. However, according to the abhidharma teachings, the four non-virtuous paths of action of speech can also be completed by causing someone else to do them.

In summary, whether we have directly done these ten non-virtuous actions, caused others to do them, or rejoiced that others have done them, these negativities are objects to be confessed.

How to Confess Negativities and Downfalls

> *Whatever karmic obscurations due to which I and sentient beings, having become obscured, will go to hell, an animal mode of rebirth, or the land of*

the hungry ghosts; will be reborn in border areas, reborn as barbarians or as long-life gods; will have imperfect faculties, hold wrong views, or will not be delighted with the arising of a buddha—in the presence of the buddha-bhagavans who are exalted wisdom, who are eyes, who are witnesses, who are valid, and who see with knowledge, I admit and confess all these karmic obscurations. I do not conceal or hide them.

Confess Negativities with Intense Regret

Among the negative actions that were explained above, if we remember having committed any of them whatsoever in this life, it is necessary to confess it with intense regret. Not only that, even if we have not committed those negativities and downfalls in this life, since we cannot certify whether we have or have not done them throughout beginningless cyclic existence up to this life, and since we have [indeed] committed those very negativities, although we do not actually remember it now, we therefore need to confess them with intense regret. Furthermore, this regret should be similar to that of, for example, having ingested poison. However, while ingesting poison does not produce anything other than the suffering of death or the suffering of merely coming close to death, having committed negativities, if they are not confessed and purified, not only will they produce the suffering of death and the suffering of coming close to death in this life but also, by the power of these karmic obscurations, we will definitely be thrown into the leisureless states (*akṣhaṇa, mi khom pa'i gnas*) in future lives.

The Result of Not Confessing Negativities—The Eight Leisureless States

If it is asked, "Well then, how many leisureless migrations projected by [these karmic obscurations] are there?" In regard to that, the root text indicates that there are the [following] eight: the three leisureless [states] with respect to the bad migrations, hell and so forth, since "will go to hell" means "will migrate to hell"; and the five leisureless [states] with respect to the happy migrations, barbarians and so forth. Moreover, being born as a long-life god is the leisureless [state] with respect to the gods. The four leisureless [states] of birth in a border

area or as a barbarian, of being dumb with imperfect faculties, of
being like the Cast-Afar (*ayata, rbyang phan pa*)[21] who hold wrong
views, and of not being delighted with the arising of a buddha in the
world—not enjoying and hating it like the malicious demons—are the
leisureless [states] with respect to humans.

The meaning of this, in brief, is that having committed a negative action,
such as one of the ten non-virtuous actions, if it is not confessed and purified, it will eventually cause us to be reborn in one of the eight leisureless
states. Leisureless, in this context, refers specifically to a lack of time and
opportunity to engage in Dharma practice.

The second link of the twelve links of dependent arising, actions or
karmic formations, includes both virtuous and non-virtuous actions. These
actions are called projecting causes because they function to project us into a
future rebirth. For example, non-virtuous actions project us into the leisureless rebirths of the lower realms as hell beings, hungry ghosts, and animals.

The leisureless state of a long-life god refers to a particular god rebirth in
a part of the fourth concentration of the form realm called Without
Discrimination. Rebirth there is due to having cultivated its specific
cause—meditation on the Absorption Without Discrimination on the basis
of calm abiding—in the immediately preceding life. At the very moment of
taking life as a long-life god, the thought occurs, "Now I am born," and
when dying, the thought occurs, "Now I am dying." Besides these two
thoughts no other mental activity occurs and these gods remain as uncon-
scious as statues for eons of time. This state is said to be without leisure
since the beings born there cannot even listen to Dharma teachings let
alone actually practice Dharma.

Four leisureless states are specified regarding rebirth as a human being. A
border area is a barbaric place in which there is no culture, written language, or religion. Birth in such a place is a leisureless state due to the total
absence of Dharma teachings. Being born with imperfect or impaired mental or sense faculties is a leisureless state because, for example, with a dull
mental faculty it would be almost impossible to practice Dharma. Our
main activities would be eating and sleeping and our life would not be
much different from that of an animal. Being born as a human but holding
wrong views like the Cast-Afar, the Hedonists, who do not accept the law

of action and result, past and future lives, etc., is said to be a leisureless state since wrong views result in a lack of interest in Dharma practice. The fourth leisureless state of human beings is usually said to be birth as a human being during a dark eon, a time when no buddha arises in the world. It is a leisureless state since without a buddha the Dharma teachings would not exist in the world and, in consequence, we would not be able to practice Dharma. Although here the root text says that the fourth leisureless state is to be unhappy like the demons with the arising of a buddha in the world, this actually means to be born in a dark eon when no buddha arises in the world.

To avoid taking rebirth in these leisureless states without the opportunity to practice the holy Dharma, we need to take care to purify each and every negativity and downfall that we have committed in this and past lives.

The Appropriateness of Confessing to the Buddha-bhagavans

> Since the buddha-bhagavans precisely realize all phenomena in general and how all our white and black actions were done in particular, they are called exalted wisdom. Moreover, since they directly and clearly see, just as eyes see forms, they are called eyes. Due to distinguishing the excellent and the faulty, the virtuous and non-virtuous actions that we have done, they are called witnesses. Having witnessed like that, since they are unmistaken and infallible in distinguishing the excellent and the faulty, they are valid persons.
>
> All the karmic obscurations mentioned above that eventually bring rebirth in the eight leisureless [states] are to be admitted and confessed in the presence of the tathāgatas who directly know and precisely see the mode in which phenomena abide, emptiness.

The buddha-bhagavans are called "exalted wisdom" because they directly realize all phenomena, everything that exists, including all our actions. They are called "eyes" because they possess the wisdom eyes that directly see, or know, whatever actions we do, both the black, negative ones as well as the white, virtuous ones. Just as we directly see the colors and shapes of visible forms with our eyes, the buddhas directly perceive all phenomena. Since they see, or witness, our non-virtuous and virtuous actions, the buddhas are also called "witnesses." They are "valid" persons due to their ability to unmistakenly and infallibly distinguish between what is right and what is wrong. Since the buddhas possess such exalted qualities, it is appropriate to confess our negativities in their presence.

Confess Negativities Openly and Honestly

The difference between admitting and confessing is that saying "admit" is telling someone, "I did this and that negativity and downfall," while, in addition to the former, saying "confess" is making a confession, by regretting what we did in the past, and a vow, by making a strong determination to restrain ourselves hereafter.

Saying "I do not conceal them"; although we have committed some kind of negativity or downfall, to not conceal it is to not entertain the wish to keep it secret from the very moment it is committed. Otherwise, it would become a negativity or downfall that is together with concealment.

Saying "I do not hide them"; like hiding stolen property in a worldly sense, to hide is to say that we have not committed a negativity or downfall that we have in fact done. Not doing so, but saying "done" with respect to the done and "not done" with respect to the not done is, when stated truthfully, to not hide it. Having committed a negativity or downfall it would be unwise to hide it because, although when hidden from someone such as a deaf mute it would not be known by him, when hidden from the perfectly complete buddhas who directly see all phenomena, since they pay attention to everything we do, any negativities and downfalls whatsoever, they would be displeased with us once more. Even if we were to commit such minor faults as digging earth, cutting grass, or drawing designs in the earth without a purpose, since the tathāgatas pay attention to it we should rely on conscientiousness by imagining ourselves as though situated in front of the tathāgatas and reflect on the inappropriateness of transgressing the advice of the sugatas. This is mentioned here because it says in *Engaging in the Bodhisattva Deeds* (*Bodhisattvacharyāvatāra, Byang chub sems dpa'i spyod pa la 'jug pa*), "I always abide in the presence of all the buddhas and bodhisattvas who are endowed with unobstructed

sight regarding all," and, "If you dig earth, cut grass, draw designs in
the earth, and so forth without a purpose, upon remembering the
advice of the sugatas, out of terror immediately give it up."

To admit our negative actions is to say, "I did such and such a negative
action" in accordance with what we have actually done. If instead we commit a negative action and then, on top of that, say that we did not do it,
this would make the buddhas, who directly see each of our actions, even
more ashamed of and displeased with us. Since the buddhas know even the
very minor faults we commit, such as the faults fully ordained monks and
nuns create through engaging in such activities as digging earth, picking or
cutting grass, or tracing designs in the earth without a specific purpose, we
should truthfully admit and purify whatever negative actions we have done.
Whether we remember them specifically or not does not matter since,
although we may not have done a specific action in this life, it is quite likely
that we have done it in a previous life. Through reflecting on this we will
develop the wish to purify each and every negative action and will therefore
put effort into the practice of confessing our negativities with the four
opponent forces.

5

The Force of Turning Away
from Faults in the Future

From now on, I will stop and refrain from them.

Not only should we confess the negativities and downfalls that we committed in the past, we should also make a firm determination to restrain ourselves from now on (i.e., hereafter), thinking, "I will desist from doing those negativities and downfalls that I have been doing and I will not do those that have not been done."

In addition to purifying the negativities already done, it is extremely important to stop committing them in the future. Saying, "From now on, I will stop and refrain from them," signifies that, although we have committed negative actions in the past, from now on we will not do them again. This firm determination, or resolution, to stop engaging in negativities is the opponent force of turning away from faults in the future. Although the text says, "I will stop and refrain from them," some teachers say that it is better to say, "I will try not to do them again," because this is likely to be more truthful. They say that if we were to promise definitely not to do a particular action again but then, some time later on, were to engage in it, our confession would become similar to a lie. However, even if, due to the strength of our afflictions, this were to happen, we should immediately apply the four opponent forces to purify the negative action.

CLOSING THE FOUR DOORS

To prevent ourselves from committing negativities in the future, we also need to close our four doors, the four means by which we continue to commit negativities. Just as, for example, if the four doors of a house are left open many unwanted things such as thieves, animals, dust, and wind can easily come inside; if we leave our four doors open we will continually engage in creating more negativities and downfalls. The four doors are (1) a lack of conscientiousness, (2) a lack of respect for others, (3) our many afflictions, and (4) a lack of knowledge. We can close these doors through applying their respective antidotes: (1) the development of mindfulness, introspection, and conscientiousness; (2) the cultivation of respect; (3) the application of a specific antidote; and (4) meditation on dependent arising and emptiness. Each of the afflictions has its own specific antidote, for example, the antidote to anger is meditation on love and compassion, the antidote to pride is analytical meditation on the eighteen constituents, and the antidote to too many thoughts is concentration on the breath. As a general antidote to all our negativities we need to cultivate the mental factors of mindfulness and introspection as this will enable us to avoid engaging in negativities and, if we find that we have engaged in them, it will enable us to purify them immediately.

The Efficacy of Purification

> In summary, the meaning of the preceding explanations is that we should put effort into confessing negativities and downfalls with intense regret by relying on all four opponent forces. If we make such an effort, no matter how many negativities and downfalls we have done in the past, through purifying them afterwards with the confession of the four forces, we will become an appropriate vessel for accomplishing the higher paths, even though our mental continuum was previously polluted by negativities and downfalls. This is like, for example, the moon that becomes beautiful due to its light in the middle of a clear sky once the cover of clouds has been cleared away. As taught in [Nāgārjuna's] *Friendly Letter* (*Suhṛllekha, bShes pa'i spring yig*), "Beautiful as the cloudless moon is one who, though once reckless, later becomes conscientious, like Nanda, Aṅgulimālā, Ajātashatru, and Shaṅkara."

To illustrate the efficacy of purification the text compares our mental continuum to the beauty of the cloud-free moon in that just as the moon in its purity is revealed when the clouds are blown way, so too the natural beauty, or purity, of our mental continuum is revealed when we purify our negative actions. Nanda, Aṅgulimālā, Ajātashatru, and Shaṅkara, each of whom was overcome by a particularly strong affliction, are mentioned to emphasize that even the strongest afflictions can be eliminated from our minds, like clouds from the sky. Nanda, a cousin of Shākyamuni Buddha, had such strong attachment for his wife that he could not bear to be separated from her for even a minute. However, through the knowledge and skill of Shākyamuni Buddha who, by his clairvoyance, perceived when the moment was ripe to subdue his cousin's mind, Nanda was able to overcome his attachment, purify his mind, and attain the state of foe-destroyer. To subdue Nanda, one day Buddha went to Nanda's house begging for alms. He gave Nanda his bowl to be filled with food but instead of accepting the filled bowl turned around and began to walk back toward his monastery. Nanda, fearing to offend the Buddha, followed with the bowl until they reached the monastery. When they entered inside, the Buddha told Nanda to have his hair cut and to take ordination as a monk. Nanda did so but, continually reminded of his beautiful wife, planned to escape from the monastery at the very first opportunity. One day his chance came but before he had gone very far he saw Buddha coming toward him and feeling ashamed he returned to the monastery. Some time later, one of Buddha's chief disciples, Maudgalyāyana, known for his magical powers, suggested to Nanda that they go for a walk together. During the walk Maudgalyāyana emanated a beautiful park in which there were many extremely attractive goddesses, each of whom was much more beautiful than Nanda's wife. Maudgalyāyana told Nanda that if he kept his vows well he would be able to enjoy the company of the goddesses in his next life. This motivated Nanda to remain in the monastery and to make more effort to keep his vows. On another occasion Maudgalyāyana, again though his psychic powers, showed Nanda a horrible place with a huge pot filled with bubbling melted iron. When Nanda questioned him about this pot, Maudgalyāyana replied that it was for a person named Nanda who would be reborn in it if he did not keep his vows purely. Nanda, very frightened by hearing this, developed strong renunciation, abandoned all attachment, completely purified his mental continuum, and eventually became a foe-destroyer.

Aṅgulimālā, a very angry person, had killed nine hundred and ninety-nine people when he met Shākyamuni Buddha. However, he too, through the skillful actions of the Buddha, was able to purify his mental continuum and become a foe-destroyer. King Ajātashatru killed his father, a highly realized being, to usurp the throne, but later he too was able to become a realized being through deeply regretting his action and engaging in purification practices. Although Shaṅkara killed his mother, he too was able to attain high realizations in that same life due to purifying his negativities. Each of these examples confirms that we too can attain the state of a holy being through striving in the practice of purification.

CONFESSION PREVENTS NEGATIVITIES FROM INCREASING

> When we confess well, the essential point of the quote, "Even the heavy negativities of the wise are light; even the light negativities of the foolish are heavy," is as though present in [the confession].

Even very heavy negativities become light when we use our wisdom and immediately apply the four opponent forces. This is because by purifying a negativity as soon as it is done, even if the action cannot be completely purified, a wise person prevents it from increasing and thereby daily becoming more and more heavy. However, the negativities of a foolish person, who thinking that it does not matter does not purify his or her negative actions, become heavy, even though initially they may have been very light. For example, if today we were to kill a single ant and did not purify this negativity, tomorrow the action would increase to equal that of having killed two ants, the next day to that of having killed four, and so on, continuing to multiply each day as long as the action is not purified. Like this, the enormity of the action continues to increase and an initially minor action becomes very serious. Consequently, it is extremely important to purify our negative actions every day since by doing so, even though we may not be able to completely purify our negative actions, at least we will be able to stop them from increasing.

THE ESSENCE OF CONFESSION

> Therefore, from the very beginning do not be stained by faults and downfalls. However, if, due to the power of the great strength of the

afflictions, you do become stained by faults and downfalls, minor and so on, it is necessary to confess them with the four forces explained previously by reciting *The Sutra of the Three Heaps.* Likewise, it is also taught in *Engaging in the Bodhisattva Deeds,* "I, with a mind fearing sorrow, having kneeled with folded hands directly in front of the Protector, confess all negativities," and, "Again and again during the day and night recite *The [Sutra of the] Three Heaps.*"

This concludes the explanation of how to confess negativities.

In conclusion, the essence of the practice of confession is, whenever you realize that you have done a negative action, to visualize the thirty-five buddhas, kneel down in front of them with your hands folded, and remembering the qualities of the Buddha, Dharma, and Sangha, go for refuge to them. Reflecting that you did such and such a negative action, and understanding that it was wrong, develop sincere regret. Then, making a firm decision to try not to do this action again, prostrate while reciting the names of the thirty-five tathāgatas. Faith and belief that this purification practice will bring beneficial results in the long run is an important factor in determining its efficacy. Do not think that you will experience the result very quickly, perhaps tomorrow or the day after tomorrow. However, by continually doing this practice you will actually purify your negative actions and eventually you will be able to achieve the realizations that lead to enlightenment.

The Bodhisattva's Confession of Downfalls is also known as *The Sutra of the Three Heaps* because it contains three heaps, or aggregates: the heap of confession, the heap of dedication, and the heap of rejoicing. The explanation of the first heap, confession, which entails the purification of negativities through the application of the four opponent forces, is concluded.

Part Two

Accumulating Merit

6

Dedicating Virtues

REQUEST THE BUDDHA-BHAGAVANS TO WITNESS THE DEDICATION

All buddha-bhagavans, please pay attention to me.

We appeal to the conquerors together with their sons, who are the thirty-five buddhas and so forth, saying, "Earlier, you very kindly witnessed my confession of negativities. Now, paying attention with great mercy, please witness my dedication."

Visualizing the buddhas and bodhisattvas in the space in front of ourselves, as is explained above, and feeling confident that they are really present even though we cannot actually see them, we appeal to them to witness our dedication. Although they are in fact present, we are unable to see them at the moment because our mind is obscured by afflictions. Upon attaining the great level of the path of accumulation we will be able to directly see, and even to communicate with, the buddhas and bodhisattvas. At that time we will also see images of the buddhas as actual emanation bodies and will be able to receive teachings directly from them. When we attain the path of seeing and become a bodhisattva superior we will see images of the buddhas as their actual enjoyment bodies. However, until then, we should feel confident that all the buddhas and bodhisattvas, in particular the thirty-five tathāgatas, are actually present in front of us. Then, with this awareness, we should respectfully request them to witness the dedication of the merit accumulated through engaging in virtuous actions in this and other lives. Through dedicating that we ourselves and all sentient beings may attain enlightenment, our merit will never be lost or exhausted until enlightenment is attained. Like putting a single drop of water into the ocean, until the ocean dries up, the drop will not dry up.

To illustrate the importance of dedicating merit, there is a traditional story of two Tibetans who met on their way to Lhasa. One man was carrying a large sack of roasted barley flour while the other had only a small sack of dark roasted pea flour. The person with the pea flour suggested to the other that they mix the two flours together, to which he kindly agreed. After some days of eating the resulting mixture the person who owned the bigger sack told the other man that the latter's portion of the flour had been consumed. However, the owner of the smaller sack disagreed and told him to take a look inside the bag of flour. Sure enough, it was possible to distinguish the darker particles of pea flour from those of the light colored barley flour. Therefore, the owner of the larger sack could not rightly claim that the other's flour had been finished. Just as the smaller sack of roasted flour is not completely consumed until the larger one is finished, likewise, when we dedicate our merit for the purpose of attaining enlightenment, due to the power of the dedication, the potential of even our smallest virtuous actions will not be consumed until every sentient being has attained enlightenment.

IDENTIFYING THE VIRTUES TO BE DEDICATED

In this life and in the other states of rebirth in which I have circled in cyclic existence throughout beginningless lives, whatever roots of virtue there are from my generosity, be it as little as having given one morsel of food to a being born in the animal realm; whatever roots of virtue there are from my having guarded morality; whatever roots of virtue there are from my pure conduct; whatever roots of virtue there are from my having fully ripened sentient beings; whatever roots of virtue there are from my having generated bodhichitta; and whatever roots of virtue there are from my unsurpassed exalted wisdom: all these, assembled and gathered, then combined together…

Thus, the virtues to be dedicated are shown to be all the roots of virtue of generosity and so forth that we have created—however many roots of virtue we have created having been illustrated with the six perfections—in this life and in the other states of rebirth in which we have circled in cyclic existence throughout beginningless lives up to this life by the power of actions and afflictions. Having said above, "all the states of rebirth in which I have circled," there is a reason for saying here, "in the other states of rebirth," because it is said like that through considering that the lives in which we created virtues are almost non-existent in comparison to the lives in which we created negativities.

If it is asked, "Well then, how are the virtues illustrated by the six perfections created?" Whatever our, the dedicators', generosity in this life and in all lifetimes, having been illustrated by the roots of virtue of the generosity of giving a small thing, a mere morsel of food, to ordinary recipients, beings in the animal realm and upwards, it also [includes] the virtues of offering all great things, our bodies, possessions, and roots of virtue, to special recipients, superiors such as the perfectly complete buddhas, as well as the generosity of Dharma of appropriately explaining the profound Dharma to the ocean-like surrounding [beings]. By showing these as virtues that are objects to be dedicated, the root text also shows the limb of offering.

Similarly, whatever roots of virtue (i.e., all whatsoever) of our having guarded morality, such as the morality of abandoning the ten non-virtues, are virtues that are objects to be dedicated.

Purity is liberation, nirvana; and pure conduct is meditating on the four immeasurables, love and so forth, for the sake of obtaining it. Moreover, [pure conduct] is the root of virtue of cultivating patience since the four immeasurables, love and so forth, destroy anger.

The [roots of] virtue of undertaking the effort that especially delights in creating virtue, indicated by saying "having fully ripened sentient beings," are the virtues of undertaking the effort that especially delights in ripening sentient beings who are not yet fully ripe and liberating those who are ripe.

The roots of virtue of cultivating concentration are generating the mind of supreme unsurpassed enlightenment and then abiding single-pointedly on it.

Unsurpassed exalted wisdom is the wisdom truth body (*jñānadharmakāya, ye shes chos sku*), while the roots of virtue of investigating the meaning of selflessness with analytical wisdom are for the sake of obtaining it.

Any of these whatsoever, that we have directly created, are virtues that are objects to be dedicated.

The objects to be dedicated are the roots of virtue created through the practice of the six perfections in this life as well as in previous lives. The commentary mentions two types of generosity in regard to the roots of virtue created through the practice of the perfection of generosity: the generosity of giving material objects and the generosity of giving the Dharma. Merely giving one mouthful of food to a being who is experiencing a bad rebirth, such as an animal, constitutes the practice of generosity and is therefore worthy of dedication. Since the practice of generosity can involve something as simple as giving a handful of grain to some birds or ants, it would seem quite easy to practice it. However, the real practice of generosity is not so much the actual action of giving as it is the development of the wish to give. It is the attitude that is completely opposite to miserliness—a tight mind and a tight fist. As such the practice of generosity also includes making mental offerings of such valuable things as our own body, possessions, and roots of virtue to special objects such as the buddhas, as well as teaching the Dharma of the vast and profound lineages to sentient beings, who are like an ocean in number and extent. By giving other people the Dharma teachings we help them to develop their knowledge, wisdom, and good qualities and to ultimately achieve every happiness. While the commentary only explicitly mentions the generosity of giving material objects and the Dharma, also the roots of virtue of having practiced the generosity of giving protection from harm and the generosity of giving love are objects to be dedicated.

The perfection of morality, like that of generosity, involves developing a particular mental attitude; in this case, the wish to completely abandon all non-virtuous actions. Three types of morality are taught: (1) the morality of abandoning, or refraining from, the ten non-virtuous actions; (2) the morality of practicing, or guarding, the ten virtuous actions; and (3) the morality of benefiting sentient beings. All the roots of virtue that we have accumulated through practicing these three types of morality, in this life and in previous lives, are objects to dedicated.

The perfection of patience is illustrated in the root text saying, "Whatever roots of virtue there are from my pure conduct." Purity is liberation or nirvana, literally the state of having gone beyond the sorrow, or suffering, of cyclic existence. To achieve this we need to create its cause, meditation on the four immeasurables: immeasurable love, compassion, joy, and equanimity. The four immeasurables are the antidotes to anger and hatred—the wish to harm sentient beings—since they are based on the wish to benefit sentient beings. For this reason, meditation on the four immeasurables is included in the perfection of patience. Whatever roots of virtue we have created by our practice of the four immeasurables in this and previous lives are therefore objects to be dedicated. When we recite the verses of the four immeasurables during our daily practices we should try to mentally generate thoughts of immeasurable love, compassion, joy, and equanimity, since by doing so we will accumulate many roots of virtue. These should be immediately dedicated for the purpose of achieving enlightenment so as to prevent anger from destroying them. Dedicating, like putting money in the bank to prevent thieves from stealing it, prevents anger from stealing away our virtues.

The roots of virtue accumulated through performing particular actions to ripen sentient beings who are not ripe and to liberate those who are ripe, are included in the perfection of joyous effort. In addition to those actions, any effort whatsoever that we put into creating virtue is included in the practice of the perfection of joyous effort. As such it is also an object to be dedicated.

The roots of virtue of generating the mind of enlightenment and then focusing on it single-pointedly are included in the perfection of concentration and are objects to be dedicated. The mind of enlightenment is composed of two aspirations, a causal aspiration and an accompanying aspiration. The causal aspiration is the great compassion that taking all sentient beings as its referent object wishes them to be free from suffering. This aspiration is the main cause for generating the mind of enlightenment. The second aspiration, the wish to attain enlightenment, accompanies the primary mind, the mind of enlightenment.

Through the practice of these five perfections—generosity, morality, patience, joyous effort, and concentration—we complete the collection of merit needed to attain the form body (*rūpakāya, gzugs sku*) of a buddha.

"Whatever roots of virtue there are from my unsurpassed exalted wisdom" refers to analytical meditation on emptiness, or selflessness, which is included in the perfection of wisdom. To attain the truth body of a buddha, we need to complete the collection of wisdom; for this purpose we meditate on emptiness. The roots of virtue thereby created are also objects to be dedicated.

In summary, all the roots of virtue accumulated through our practice of the six perfections are objects to be dedicated.

Dedicating Our Own and Others' Virtues

> Then, if it is asked, "What is the difference between the three, 'assembled,' 'gathered,' and 'combined together'?" The difference between the three is like this. Saying "assembled" indicates, "All the virtues I have created in the three times are assembled into a group." "Gathered" is an old term, which in new terminology means assembled. It indicates that the virtues accumulated in the three times by other beings are also assembled into a group. "Combined together" indicates that both the virtues created by ourselves and the virtues created by others, combined together, are the virtues to be dedicated to complete enlightenment.

"Assembled" indicates that the virtues that we ourselves have created in the three times—past, present, and future—are collected into a group. "Gathered" indicates that the virtues created in the three times by all other beings are also collected into a group. "Combined together" indicates that our own collection of virtues as well as the collections of virtues of all other sentient beings are brought together and then dedicated to enlightenment. Consequently, the objects to be dedicated include both our own collection of virtues as well as that of every other sentient being. By dedicating in this way the practice of dedication becomes very effective.

> I offer this king of wish-fulfilling jewels, a highly cherished system of explanation from the treasury of excellent explanations, to my guru in order to repay his kindness.

How to Dedicate

> *I totally dedicate to the unsurpassed, the unexcelled, that higher than the high, that superior to the superior; thereby, do I totally dedicate to*

unsurpassed, perfectly complete enlightenment.

Just as the buddha-bhagavans of the past totally dedicated, just as the buddha-bhagavans of the future will totally dedicate, and just as the buddha-bhagavans presently abiding totally dedicate, I too similarly totally dedicate.

A fervent aspiration will arise at the beginning of making a dedication when we excellently connect [the objects to be dedicated with the aim of the dedication]. Although in general there are many ways of dedicating, the supreme and perfect ways of connecting them are (1) dedication as a cause of the flourishing of the doctrine, the source of benefit and happiness; (2) dedication as a cause of being cared for by a guru, the source of attainments; and (3) dedication to unsurpassed complete enlightenment.

Furthermore, dedicating as a cause of the flourishing of the doctrine is considered an unsurpassed dedication, since in dependence on the survival of the doctrine we become manifestly completely enlightened and then solely enact the welfare of others, such as accomplishing the benefit and happiness of all sentient beings. Also, dedicating as a cause of being cared for by holy gurus is considered an unsurpassed dedication since all temporal and ultimate qualities depend on the holy guru and by dedicating virtues in this way we will be gladly cared for by holy gurus in all our lives, in dependence upon which all qualities will arise. Also, as taught in *The Stages of the Path*, dedicating to unsurpassed complete enlightenment is considered an unsurpassed dedication because, just as, for example, when for the purpose of growing barley or rice, we plant their seeds and, even though unwanted, the stalks arise, likewise, when we dedicate virtues for the purpose of attaining unsurpassed complete enlightenment, incidentally, all other qualities will arise. Therefore, my holy guru, the lord of wisdom, glorious Tsongkhapa, having seen this powerful fact, also dedicated every virtue to all these dedications, any of the three. Among the ways of dedicating, in this context the dedication is to complete enlightenment.

Furthermore, [the root text] states "the unsurpassed" and "the unexcelled." Although unsurpassed and unexcelled are, in general, synonymous, here it is not considered to be an error to state both because "the unsurpassed" indicates the form body while "the unexcelled" indicates the truth body. The difference between saying "that higher than the high" and "that superior to the superior" is also similar because "that higher than the high" indicates the enjoyment body and "that superior to the superior" indicates the emanation body. There is a reason for calling the enjoyment body "that higher than the high," because "the high" is said in regard to the bodhisattvas on the tenth ground, while the enjoyment body is higher than the bodhisattvas on the tenth ground. There is a reason for calling the emanation body "that superior to the superior," because "the superior" is said in regard to the hearer and solitary realizer foe-destroyers and the bodhisattvas abiding on the pure grounds, while the emanation body is superior even to them.

Who has formerly seen or heard an explanation like this? It has excellently come forth thus from the compassion of the deity and the guru.

Therefore, since the virtues explained previously are dedicated for the purpose of attaining the form body and the truth body, this is the meaning of saying, "I totally dedicate to unsurpassed, perfectly complete enlightenment." Moreover, just as, for example, the previous buddha-bhagavans of the past dedicated virtues to complete enlightenment, just as the buddha-bhagavans of the future will also dedicate, and just as the buddha-bhagavans presently abiding are totally dedicating virtues to complete enlightenment, we too similarly totally dedicate virtues to complete enlightenment.

The best type of dedication is the dedication to complete enlightenment, praying that our virtuous actions become the cause for ourselves and all sentient beings to achieve enlightenment—the truth and form bodies, or the holy mind and holy body, of a buddha. However, we can also dedicate to the flourishing and abiding of the doctrine, to always being cared for in all our lives by holy gurus, or in fact to any virtuous purpose whatsoever. In short, we should dedicate our virtues in the same way as the buddhas of the past dedicated, as the future buddhas will dedicate, and as the present buddhas are dedicating.

Take Care to Dedicate

We should take great care to dedicate our virtues to complete enlightenment because the lord of yogis, Milarepa, taught, "The two, a great meditator meditating in a cave and the benefactor who supplies him with the necessities of life, have the auspiciousness of equally serving to awaken," and, "How is there auspiciousness? The heart of auspiciousness is dedication. Afterwards, take care to dedicate." By dedicating virtues—illustrated by the virtues of supplying the necessities of life—as the cause of attaining buddhahood, we will attain buddhahood through the auspiciousness of having dedicated to it. [Milarepa] also said to disciples who came later, "After you have created virtue, take care in the dedication."

To emphasize the importance of making a dedication after every virtuous action, Milarepa gave the example of a meditator in a cave and the person providing his needs, both of whom dedicate their actions for the purpose of attaining enlightenment. Due to the power of the dedication—the cause—both the meditator and the benefactor create the auspiciousness (*pratītyasamutpāda, rten 'brel*), or the dependent relation, to simultaneously attain buddhahood, the result.

In fact, the teachings on mind training (*blo sbyong*) state that two things are important in regard to creating virtuous actions. At the beginning of the action it is important to generate a good motivation and at its conclusion it is important to dedicate the virtue created. If we do both of these we can collect many virtues, since even our daily actions of eating, drinking, sleeping, walking, dressing, and washing can be transformed into virtuous actions when done with a good motivation. If we practice like this, whatever we do will be done with the good intention of benefiting others. Just as, for example, the bodhisattvas who follow the sutra teachings eat and drink with the intention of nourishing the many thousands of tiny organisms that live within their bodies, we too should likewise try to practice generosity. Alternatively, if we are mainly practicing tantra we can practice generosity through offering our food and drink to our guru visualized at our heart as inseparable from the deity.

In brief, at the moment we have a human body with eighteen special qualities that is better than a wish-fulfilling jewel; however, it is extremely difficult to obtain again. Therefore, rejoicing in how fortunate we are, we should use this body to the best of our ability to benefit other sentient beings as well as ourselves. Rather than using it as if it were a vessel containing negativities, we should use it to become a pure vessel of the perfections of generosity, morality, patience, joyous effort, concentration, and wisdom.

7

The Seven Limbs

I confess all negativities individually.
I rejoice in all merit.
I urge and request all buddhas.
May I attain the supreme excellence of unsurpassed exalted wisdom.

The meaning of "I confess all negativities individually," is [the follow-ing]: since negativities accumulated by way of the body need to be confessed by prostrations and so forth; since negativities accumulated by way of the speech need to be confessed by saying the names of the tathāgatas, reciting profound mantra-dharanis (*dhāraṇī, gzungs sngags*),[22] and so forth; and since negativities accumulated by way of the mind need to be confessed by way of meditating on the path; this is elucidated saying, "I confess them individually."

"I confess all negativities individually" shows the limb of confessing the negativities, that were indicated above, and the limb of offering through combining them together. In addition to these two, [the root text] shows the limb of rejoicing in all merit, the virtues created by our-selves and others; the limb of urging all the buddhas of the ten direc-tions to turn the wheel of Dharma; the limb of requesting them to not show the aspect of passing beyond sorrow but to remain as long as the eons are not emptied; and, having summarized the ways of dedicating explained above by saying, "May I attain the supreme excellence of unsurpassed exalted wisdom," it shows the limb of dedication. We should thereby understand that the seven limbs are shown in their entirety.

The Sutra of the Bodhisattva's Confession of Downfalls includes the entire seven-limb prayer, an essential method for purifying negativities and accumulating merit. The first limb, the limb of prostration was explained earlier in regard to the lines of the root text, "I prostrate to Tathāgata...." Since physical prostrations purify the negativities created by the body; recitation of the names of the thirty-five tathāgatas purifies the negativities created by the speech; and meditation on, or related to, the path—love, compassion, emptiness, the four immeasurables, and so forth—purifies the negativities created by the mind; it is important to do all three together.

The second limb, the limb of offering, was explained as being implicitly included in the root text in both the lines of prostration, "I prostrate to Tathāgata...," as well as in the dedication of the roots of virtue of generosity. We can make various types of offerings, such as the four types of offerings taught in tantra, the outer, inner, secret, and suchness offerings. As explained previously the outer offerings are both actual material substances and mentally imagined ones. The inner offering, according to highest yoga tantra, is composed of ten impure substances transformed into nectar. The secret offering is the offering of bliss to our guru who is visualized as inseparable from the deity. The suchness offering is the offering of our realization of emptiness.

The third limb, confession, involves the application of the four opponent forces to purify our negativities. The fourth limb, rejoicing, specifically refers to the practice of rejoicing in our own and others' virtuous actions. The fifth limb is the limb of urging that urges, or exhorts, the buddhas to turn the wheel of Dharma—in other words to teach the Dharma. The sixth, the limb of requesting, requests all the buddhas to not pass away. These six limbs serve to accumulate virtues that are then dedicated, together with other virtuous actions created by ourselves and others, in order that we and all other sentient beings may attain enlightenment. This is the seventh limb, that of dedication.

Each of the seven limbs also functions to reduce a particular mental affliction. The limb of prostration is the antidote to pride; presenting offerings is the antidote to miserliness; confession is the antidote to the three mental poisons, attachment, hatred, and ignorance; rejoicing is the antidote to jealousy; urging the buddhas to turn the wheel of Dharma is the antidote to having abandoned the Dharma in the past; and requesting them to not pass away is the antidote to negative actions committed in relation to our guru. Therefore, with this one simple practice we can purify eons of negativities and accumulate a huge amount of merit.

> The light rays of the compassion of the deity and guru have caused the lotus of intelligence to excellently blossom, producing this new system of explanation, the essence of honey, that I have now revealed. How wonderful!

This sutra is also called *The Sutra of the Three Heaps* because it was explained as such since it expresses the three: the heap of confessing negativities, the heap of dedicating virtues, and the heap of rejoicing.

GOING FOR REFUGE TO THE THREE JEWELS AGAIN

> *To the best of humans, the conquerors who are presently abiding, those of the past, and likewise those of the future, to all those whose exalted qualities are like an infinite ocean, folding my hands, I approach for refuge.*

Having explicitly shown, "Folding my hands (i.e., venerating them), I approach (i.e., go) for refuge to the conquerors who are the best of humans—the buddhas who are presently abiding; the buddhas of the past (i.e., those who already came before); and, likewise, the buddhas of the future—with their infinite qualities of body, speech, and mind, the infinitely praised, all the buddhas of the three times who are like a great ocean," it implicitly shows going for refuge to the Dharma Jewel and the Sangha Jewel.

At the end of the prayer we go for refuge once again to the Three Jewels saying, "Folding my hands, I approach for refuge." This implies placing our complete trust in the Buddha, Dharma, and Sangha.

SIGNS OF PURIFICATION

> When confessing negativities and downfalls by means of the seven limbs, there is a manner in which signs [of purification] occur in dreams. It is taught in *The Dharani That Exhorts* (*Chuṇḍādhāraṇī,*

bsKul byed kyi gzungs), that signs in dreams of purifying negativities are vomiting bad food; drinking yogurt, milk, and so on; seeing the sun or the moon; traveling in the sky; [seeing] a blazing fire; defeating a buffalo or a person [wearing] black; seeing a sangha of fully ordained monks or nuns; climbing a tree spouting milk; mounting an elephant or a bull; climbing a mountain, a lion throne, or a mansion; listening to the Dharma; and so forth.

If we recite the names of the thirty-five buddhas while doing prostrations and at the same time generate the four opponent forces in our mind, we will experience great benefit. Signs in dreams of, for example, vomiting bad food, drinking white liquids such as milk or yogurt, wearing white clothes, and so on, confirm that we are successfully purifying our negativities.

Part Three

Conclusion

8

Overcoming the Afflictions

ANALYZE HOW AFFLICTIONS ARISE

In addition to confessing negativities it is also extremely important to analyze how the various afflictions arise in your mind. This analysis enables us to apply their respective antidotes before they lead us to engage in negative actions. For example, examine how attachment, one of the strongest mental afflictions, arises in your mind. You will find that whenever you come into contact with an attractive object, immediately and automatically attachment arises. For example, when you smell the pleasant odor of food cooking, the attachment of wishing to eat it arises. When you hear good music, immediately something in your mind awakens and attachment arises. When you see attractively designed clothes, immediately attachment follows and you think "I like that. I want it."

Anger, or hatred, is another of our strongest afflictions. It arises when we come into contact with people or objects that we consider unpleasant. Although anger is not always present, when certain conditions come together it easily arises. If we examine our mind well, we will probably find that, like most ordinary people, we get angry as often as once a day, if not more often.

Another of our root, or principal, afflictions is ignorance. Ignorance is the main cause of all our problems because a lack of knowledge and understanding leads us to easily make many mistakes. The result of these mistakes is problems, difficulties, and a lot of suffering.

Another affliction is pride; for example, the pride that thinks, "I am beautiful," "I am very good," or "I am very skillful." Pride causes us to become swollen up with ourselves.

Doubt, the inability to make a decision, is also present in our mental continuum. Doubt causes us to think, "Maybe yes. Maybe no. Maybe this.

Maybe that." It becomes a cause of problems when it continually interferes with our ability to come to a decision and thereby prevents us from achieving success in any of our undertakings.

Jealousy is another very harmful affliction. If we examine how it arises we will find that when something nice happens to another person, jealousy automatically arises in our mind. For example, if we see our boyfriend or girlfriend talking with someone else, immediately we want to know why he or she is talking to that person. We begin to suspect that he or she is planning to leave us and start a relationship with that other person. Consequently, jealousy is the cause of disharmony in our relationships and brings us many problems in our day-to-day life.

You should check to see whether or not you have these afflictions in your mental continuum. You will probably find that almost all of the root and secondary afflictions are present, except perhaps, some of the wrong views such as holding an inferior view as supreme or holding bad conduct and bad morality as supreme. However, even though we may not have those particular afflictions, we have many other afflictions in our mind and consequently we need to purify them.

APPLY THE SPECIFIC ANTIDOTES TO THE AFFLICTIONS

The afflictions are our enemies because they harm us, not only by disturbing our present peace of mind, but also by causing us to engage in negative actions that eventually result in suffering. However, although our main enemies are within our own mind, generally we do not recognize this fact and, instead, point to our enemy as being someone external to ourselves. We consider someone to be our enemy if he or she has harmed us, our friends, or our relatives. Considering our afflictions using the same line of reasoning, we will see that our negative emotions are our real enemies, since they can bring us much more harm than any external enemy. To destroy the inner enemies of the afflictions, we have no need of physical weapons, only the development of our own inner qualities serves to accomplish their destruction.

We need to apply specific antidotes to each of the various afflictions. By doing so, the strength of our afflictions gradually diminishes and we will become much more relaxed and happy. This is the tangible result of our Dharma practice, the employing of methods to improve and develop our mind. We have two types of mind—quality mind and faulty mind. We need to purify the faulty mind and develop the quality mind. In this way, we will gain the realizations of a bodhisattva. *Sattva* means "person" or "being," while *bodhi* means "big mind" or "big heart"; therefore, a bodhisattva is a being with a big heart who wishes to attain complete enlightenment for the benefit of all sentient beings.

Anger. The method to diminish our afflictions is meditation. For example, if anger is our main problem, we need to engage in doing specific meditations that develop compassion and love. When we are angry we have the wish to harm, to beat, to hit, to insult. As a remedy we need to develop compassion and love, the main causes of our mental peace and relaxation.

Compassion is the attitude wishing that all sentient beings could be free from suffering. We meditate in order to make this attitude manifest, to transform our mind into the nature of compassion. Having accomplished this, we try to hold this attitude in our mind and focus upon it. However, it will probably quickly disappear and we will find that we need to make an effort to develop it once again. At first the compassion we generate will last only a minute, or maybe just a second, but by developing it again and again it will come to last for five minutes, ten minutes, fifteen minutes, and so on, gradually becoming more and more stable. By making a constant effort day after day, some result will definitely come—the hatred and anger will lessen and we will gradually find ourselves becoming more patient and relaxed.

We can also meditate on love to overcome anger. In this context, love does not refer to the kind of love we mean when we say, "I love you." Generally, when we say "I love you," we mean "I am attached to you." Real love is the mental attitude wishing that all sentient beings have happiness. Through meditation we make this kind of mind manifest, we transform our mind into the nature of love and then hold and focus on this attitude. This is what is known as meditation on love.

Attachment. Attachment arises through exaggerating the good qualities of a particular object. At first we may think that the object is beautiful, then that it is the most beautiful. Thinking this way, our attachment for the object grows. If we examine how we react to attractive objects we will see that we have had this experience many times. Then, when we are unable to acquire the desired object, we become unhappy and suffer. To diminish our attachment to an object, we can meditate to diminish its beautiful appearance and to see it in its reality. If we are unable to do this, as Vasubandhu says in the *Abhidharmakosha*, the best way for ordinary people to reduce attachment is to put a distance between themselves and the object. This distance can be physical, mental, or both. Physical distance implies staying away from the object. Mental distance means to stop thinking about the object of attachment. If we are able do this the manifest attachment for that object will gradually diminish.

Ignorance. There are various antidotes to ignorance, one of which is the meditation analyzing how phenomena exist as dependent relations. An example of a dependent relation is the appearance of a particular person as our enemy that arises in dependence upon our considering him or her an enemy. Since this appearance arose in dependence upon our own point of view, we can work to change our way of thinking. From our own side we can make an effort to become friends with that person and thereby bring about a transformation in the relationship. In fact, whether we have a good or bad relationship with a specific person depends entirely upon ourselves.

It is essential to understand how everything exists as a dependent relation, or dependent arising. By way of this realization, we come to understand the final, or ultimate, nature of all phenomena—emptiness (*shūnyatā, stong pa nyid*). The realization of emptiness is called wisdom (*prajñā, shes rab*) or mother. The mind of enlightenment, great compassion, is called method (*upaya, thabs*) or father. The union of mother and father, wisdom and method, the realization of emptiness and bodhichitta, gives birth to the child of a buddha, a bodhisattva.

There are many different types of ignorance. The ignorance that is the root of cyclic existence is the ignorance that grasps at a truly, or inherently, existing self. The main antidote to this ignorance is the wisdom realizing emptiness. Emptiness means that a self of persons and a self of phenomena lack inherent existence, they are empty of true existence. This realization destroys self-grasping, the grasping at an inherently existing self, the source of all our other afflictions. Therefore, it is extremely important to meditate on emptiness.

During meditation on emptiness we first develop an image of emptiness in our mind and then focus on it. Consequently, at first it is only a mental image, a mere reflection of actual emptiness. By continuing to meditate on emptiness using a specific process of analysis, the image gradually becomes more and more clear until eventually we realize emptiness by way of a direct perceiver (*pratyaksha, mngon sum*). At this point emptiness is understood directly without any further need to use reasoning, just as we directly see an object held in our hand.

Pride. Through understanding dependent relation we are able to understand that all phenomena do not inherently exist. Why do they not inherently exist? Only because they exist as dependent relations. We should use this reasoning to analyze the mode of existence of the self or I. For example, when we think, "I know everything," pride arises. To reduce this pride we should examine where, and what, is this I. We begin by checking whether the form aggregate, our body, is I. If the body is I then which part of it is I? The head, the arms, the legs...? Nowhere in the body do we find an I. Our body is a collection of eight types of atoms: those of the four root elements (earth, water, fire, and wind) and those of the four secondary elements (visible form, odor, taste, and tangible object). Which of these is I? Again we find that none of them is I. Why? If this body were I, then the I would continue to exist in our corpse when we die. However, it is not so.

Next check whether or not the feeling aggregate is I. If it seems to be I, is the I pleasant, unpleasant, or neutral feeling? Then check whether the discrimination aggregate is the I. Examine whether it is the wrong discrimination that discriminates the impermanent as permanent, the suffering as happiness, the impure as pure, and the selfless as having a self. Or is it the right discrimination that discriminates these four correctly? Check the compositional factors aggregate for the I. Forty-nine mental factors and fourteen non-associated compositional factors are included in this aggregate. Is it one of them? We will find that none of the feelings, discriminations, or compositional factors are I.

Finally, check the consciousness aggregate to determine whether or not it is I. Is the eye, ear, nose, tongue, body, or mental consciousness I? Is virtuous mind, non-virtuous mind, or neutral mind I? In this way, we should examine the five aggregates and the eighteen constituents for the I, the self.

However, even though we may check, we will not find an I. There is no concrete "beautiful I" or "knowledgeable I." We can look for it but it cannot be found. Reflect on this. Doing this type of analytical meditation reduces pride.

Doubt. Doubt often arises in our minds. In order to counteract it we can do one of many different kinds of breathing meditations. For example, focus your mind on the breath as you inhale and exhale and, with a part of the mind, count each cycle from one up to twenty-one. This meditation functions to diminish the thoughts, or conceptions, arising in our minds. Another type of breathing meditation is to imagine that as you exhale you breathe out black smoke which is in the nature of all your doubts, worries, afflictions, sicknesses, and unhappiness. When you inhale imagine that your breath has the aspect of white light which is in the nature of all the qualities of the holy beings, their love, compassion, energy, and wisdom, as well as all the good energy in the universe from the mountains, lakes, oceans, and trees. Imagine that you receive the blessings of all the holy beings and let your mind become completely relaxed. If you find that your mind is very disturbed by many thoughts, put the emphasis on the visualization of exhaling black smoke, your negative energy. When your mind is more relaxed put the emphasis on receiving the positive energy of all the holy beings.

Although there are many different breathing meditations, all of them involve applying a particular antidote to our negative emotions. There is real benefit from doing this type of meditation. Just as your stomach discomfort is finished when you succeed in vomiting up the food that caused the problem, imagine that by expelling all your negative energy your mental disturbance finishes and your mind becomes quiet and relaxed. This type of meditation provides one of the conditions for our positive energy to develop and increase.

However, although meditation on the breath is one way to reduce doubt, the main antidote to doubt is the development of wisdom. The more wisdom we develop, the less doubt will arise.

Jealousy. As mentioned previously, rejoicing in the good qualities, actions, and fortune of others is the main antidote to jealousy. Rejoicing is a mind that delights in others' happiness and as such is completely opposite to the mind of jealousy. Through rejoicing we create the cause to experience that happiness ourselves in the future.

In conclusion, put effort into purifying your negative actions using a method such as *The Bodhisattva's Confession of Downfalls* and strive to overcome your mental afflictions by meditating on their specific antidotes. By doing so, gradually all your faults will diminish and all your qualities will increase.

9

Final Dedications

Sanggye Yeshe's Dedication

This is mentioned here from the compassion of all the gurus along with the deities. I, Buddhajñāna (*Sangs rgyas ye shes*), a saffron-robed individual liberation being, wrote down in script this excellent account explaining a mere portion of the meaning of the profound *Sutra of the Three Heaps* for the purpose of delighting the fortunate ones of new awareness. Due to whatever collection of pristine virtues has arisen from it, may the negativities and downfalls, together with their imprints, accumulated continuously in life after life from beginningless time by myself and the kind ones, be cleansed and purified and then, may we quickly attain the ultimate—buddhahood that is free from obscurations and complete in all qualities. Also, temporally, may the day and night be filled with the light of benefit and happiness from the rising of a pair, the sun and the moon of study and practice, the means of spreading and developing the precious doctrine of the Subduer in all directions and times.

I, faithfully and devoutly, request the gurus together with the deities, as well as the hosts of scholars, to forgive whatever faults I have made in composing this method. Please mercifully let me be without obscurations.

The Sutra of the Three Heaps is like a door blocking negative ones like myself from falling into an abyss. Having abandoned stains of errors in the words and meaning, close the door to the lower realms. Fortunate ones, abide joyfully. Be faithful by having seen the heroes that destroy doubt. Prostrate to the treasures of compassion, the assembly of thirty-five tathāgatas. Upon hearing their names the unbearable sufferings of cyclic existence, without an exception, are destroyed in a single instant.

The Sutra of The Confession of Downfalls with the four forces in their entirety is the best of antidotes to the eighty-four thousand afflictions.

THE SPONSOR'S DEDICATION

This source of attainments clarifying the words and meanings was printed due to me, Samdrub Tsering (*bsam grub tshe ring*). Due to these virtues may the precious doctrine spread and flourish. May the lotus feet of the holy doctrine holders without exception be firm. May my parents and relatives be victorious in the battle with the two obscurations and may they each accomplish every aim of this and future [lives]. For the sake of eliminating the torment of migrators, I devoutly offer this excellent explanation, medicine for migrators, to Tse [Chog] Ling with a mind of benefiting migrators, for the purpose of augmenting the welfare of migrators.

Appendices

The above diagram corresponds to the placement of the figures in the cover thangka of the thirty-five confession buddhas. The numbers correspond to the order in which the buddhas are enumerated in the prayer, *The Bodhisattva's Confession of Downfalls*.

1

The Bodhisattva's Confession of Downfalls

I, (*say your name*), for all time, go for refuge to the guru;
I go for refuge to the Buddha;
I go for refuge to the Dharma;
I go for refuge to the Sangha.

I prostrate to [Teacher] Bhagavan Tathāgata Foe-Destroyer Perfectly
    Complete Buddha Glorious Conqueror Shākyamuni.
I prostrate to Tathāgata Thoroughly Destroying With Vajra Essence.
I prostrate to Tathāgata Radiant Jewel.
I prostrate to Tathāgata Nāga-Lord King.
I prostrate to Tathāgata Army of Heroes.
I prostrate to Tathāgata Delighted Hero.
I prostrate to Tathāgata Jewel Fire.
I prostrate to Tathāgata Jewel Moonlight.
I prostrate to Tathāgata Meaningful to Behold.
I prostrate to Tathāgata Jewel Moon.
I prostrate to Tathāgata Immaculate.
I prostrate to Tathāgata Bestowed With Courage.
I prostrate to Tathāgata Purity.
I prostrate to Tathāgata Bestowed With Purity.
I prostrate to Tathāgata Water-God.
I prostrate to Tathāgata Water-God Deity.
I prostrate to Tathāgata Glorious Excellence.
I prostrate to Tathāgata Glorious Sandalwood.
I prostrate to Tathāgata Infinite Splendor.
I prostrate to Tathāgata Glorious Light.
I prostrate to Tathāgata Glorious Sorrowless.

I prostrate to Tathāgata Son of Cravingless.
I prostrate to Tathāgata Glorious Flower.
I prostrate to Tathāgata Pure Light Rays Clearly Knowing by Sporting.
I prostrate to Tathāgata Lotus Light Rays Clearly Knowing by Sporting.
I prostrate to Tathāgata Glorious Wealth.
I prostrate to Tathāgata Glorious Mindfulness.
I prostrate to Tathāgata Glorious Name Widely Renowned.
I prostrate to Tathāgata Most Powerful Victory Banner King.
I prostrate to Tathāgata Glorious Utterly Suppressing.
I prostrate to Tathāgata Totally Victorious in Battle.
I prostrate to Tathāgata Glorious Suppressing Advancement.
I prostrate to Tathāgata Glorious All-Illuminating Manifestations.
I prostrate to Tathāgata Jewel Lotus Suppresser.
I prostrate to Tathāgata Foe-Destroyer Perfectly Complete Buddha
   Mountain Lord King Firmly Seated on Jewels and a Lotus.

These and others, as many tathāgata foe-destroyer perfectly complete buddha-bhagavans as are abiding, living, and residing in all the world systems of the ten directions, all buddha-bhagavans, please pay attention to me.

In this life and in all the states of rebirth in which I have circled in cyclic existence throughout beginningless lives, whatever negative actions I have done, caused to be done, or rejoiced in the doing of; whatever possessions of stupas, possessions of the sangha, or possessions of the sangha of the ten directions I have appropriated, made to be appropriated, or rejoiced in the appropriation of; whatever of the five actions of immediate [retribution] I have done, caused to be done, or rejoiced in the doing of; whatever of the ten non-virtuous paths of action I have engaged in the adoption of, caused to be engaged in, or rejoiced in the engagement in; whatever karmic obscurations due to which I and sentient beings, having become obscured, will go to hell, an animal mode of rebirth, or the land of the hungry ghosts, will be reborn in border areas, reborn as barbarians or as long-life gods, will have imperfect faculties, hold wrong views, or will not be delighted with the arising of a buddha—in the presence of the buddha-bhagavans who are exalted wisdom, who are eyes, who are witnesses, who are valid, and who see with knowledge, I admit and confess all these karmic obscurations. I do not conceal or hide them. From now on, I will stop and refrain from them.

All buddha-bhagavans please pay attention to me. In this life and in the other states of rebirth in which I have circled in cyclic existence throughout beginningless lives, whatever roots of virtue there are from my generosity, be it as little as having given one morsel of food to a being born in the animal realm; whatever roots of virtue there are from my having guarded morality; whatever roots of virtue there are from my pure conduct; whatever roots of virtue there are from my having fully ripened sentient beings; whatever roots of virtue there are from my having generated bodhichitta; and whatever roots of virtue there are from my unsurpassed exalted wisdom: all these, assembled and gathered, then combined together, I totally dedicate to the unsurpassed, the unexcelled, that higher than the high, that superior to the superior; thereby, do I totally dedicate to unsurpassed, perfectly complete enlightenment.

Just as the buddha-bhagavans of the past totally dedicated, just as the buddha-bhagavans of the future will totally dedicate, and just as the buddha-bhagavans presently abiding totally dedicate, I too similarly totally dedicate.

I confess all negativities individually.
I rejoice in all merit.
I urge and request all buddhas.
May I attain the supreme excellence of unsurpassed exalted wisdom.

To the best of humans, the conquerors who are presently abiding, those of the past, and likewise those of the future, to all those whose exalted qualities are like an infinite ocean, folding my hands, I approach for refuge.

2

Woodblock Prints
of the Thirty-five Tathāgatas

The following woodblock prints are believed to have originally come from a Nyingma text titled *Dharma Treasure of the Confession of All Negativities: A Golden Razor for Confessing Negativities* (*sDigs bShags gSer gyi sPu gri*), and accord quite closely with the cover thangka of the thirty-five tathāgatas.

The images of the woodblock prints do not correspond directly with the descriptions of the thirty-five buddhas from Lama Tsongkhapa's vision, as explained in his text *Practice of the Thirty-five Buddhas and a Description of the Deities' Bodies* (see chart on pp. 38–39). Although the mudras depicted in these prints may differ, according to advice from Geshe Jampa Gyatso one can still visualize the individual buddhas according to their colors as described in Lama Tsongkhapa's text.

These woodblock prints have been included in the hope that readers will derive benefit from them in their personal visualization practice.

Tathāgata Foe-Destroyer
Perfectly Complete Buddha
Glorious Conqueror
Shākyamuni

Tathāgata Thoroughly
Destroying
With Vajra Essence

Tathāgata Radiant Jewel

Tathāgata Nāga-Lord King

Tathāgata Army of Heroes

Tathāgata Delighted Hero

Tathāgata Jewel Fire

Tathāgata Jewel Moonlight

Tathāgata Meaningful
to Behold

ཀྲུ་བ་རིན་ཆེན་ཟླ་བ་ལ་འདུད་དོ།

Tathāgata Jewel Moon

ཀྲུ་བ་དྲི་མ་མེད་པ་ལ་འདུད་དོ།

Tathāgata Immaculate

ཀྲུ་བ་དཔའ་སྦྱིན་ལ་འདུད་དོ།

Tathāgata Bestowed
With Courage

ཀྲུ་བ་གཙང་བ་ལ་འདུད་དོ།

Tathāgata Purity

ཀྲུ་བ་གཙང་བས་སྦྱིན་ལ་འདུད་དོ།

Tathāgata Bestowed
With Purity

ཀྲུ་བ་ཆུ་ལྷ་ལ་འདུད་དོ།

Tathāgata Water-God

ཀྲུ་བ་ཆུ་ལྷའི་ལྷ་ལ་འདུད་དོ།

Tathāgata Water-God Deity

ཀྲུ་བ་དཔལ་བཟང་ལ་འདུད་དོ།

Tathāgata Glorious
Excellence

ཀྲུ་བ་ཙན་དན་དཔལ་ལ་འདུད་དོ།

Tathāgata Glorious
Sandalwood

Tathāgata Infinite Splendor   Tathāgata Glorious Light   Tathāgata Glorious
Sorrowless

Tathāgata Son
of Cravingless   Tathāgata Glorious Flower   Tathāgata Pure Light
Rays Clearly Knowing
by Sporting

Tathāgata Lotus Light Rays
Clearly Knowing
by Sporting   Tathāgata Glorious Wealth   Tathāgata Glorious
Mindfulness

Tathāgata Glorious Name Widely Renowned

Tathāgata Most Powerful Victory Banner King

Tathāgata Glorious Utterly Suppressing

Tathāgata Totally Victorious in Battle

Tathāgata Glorious Suppressing Advancement

Tathāgata Glorious All-Illuminating Manifestations

Tathāgata Jewel Lotus Suppresser

Tathāgata Foe-Destroyer Perfectly Complete Buddha Mountain Lord King Firmly Seated on Jewels and a Lotus

3

Phonetics *of* The Bodhisattva's Confession of Downfalls

Dag (*say your name*) zhe gyi wa
Dü tag tu la ma la kyab su chi o
Sang gye la kyab su chi o
Chö la kyab su chi o
Gen dun la kyab su chi o

Tön pa chom den de de zhin sheg pa dra chom pa yang dag par dzog pe sang
gye pel gyel wa sha kya tub pa la chag tsel lo
De zhin sheg pa *dor je nying pö rab tu jom pa* la chag tsel lo
De zhin sheg pa *rin chen ö tro* la chag tsel lo
De zhin sheg pa *lu wang gi gyel po* la chag tsel lo
De zhin sheg pa *pa wö de* la chag tsel lo
De zhin sheg pa *pel gye* la chag tsel lo
De zhin sheg pa *rin chen me* la chag tsel lo
De zhin sheg pa *rin chen da ö* la chag tsel lo
De zhin sheg pa *tong wa dön yö* la chag tsel lo
De zhin sheg pa *rin chen da wa* la chag tsel lo
De zhin sheg pa *dri ma me pa* la chag tsel lo
De zhin sheg pa *pel jin* la chag tsel lo
De zhin sheg pa *tsang pa* la chag tsel lo
De zhin sheg pa *tsang pe jin* la chag tsel lo
De zhin sheg pa *chu hla* la chag tsel lo
De zhin sheg pa *chu hle hla* la chag tsel lo
De zhin sheg pa *pel zang* la chag tsel lo
De zhin sheg pa *tzen den pel* la chag tsel lo

De zhin sheg pa *zi ji ta ye* la chag tsel lo
De zhin sheg pa *ö pel* la chag tsel lo
De zhin sheg pa *nya ngen me pe pel* la chag tsel lo
De zhin sheg pa *se me kyi bu* la chag tsel lo
De zhin sheg pa *me tog pel* la chag tsel lo
De zhin sheg pa *tsang pe ö zer nam par röl pe ngön par kyen pa* la chag tsel lo
De zhin sheg pa *pe me ö zer nam par röl pe ngön par kyen pa* la chag tsel lo
De zhin sheg pa *nor pel* la chag tsel lo
De zhin sheg pa *dren pe pel* la chag tsel lo
De zhin sheg pa *tsen pel shin tu yong drag* la chag tsel lo
De zhin sheg pa *wang pö tog gi gyel tsen gyi gyel po* la chag tsel lo
De zhin sheg pa *shin tu nam par nön pe pel* la chag tsel lo
De zhin sheg pa *yül le shin tu nam par gyel wa* la chag tsel lo
De zhin sheg pa *nam par nön pe sheg pe pel* la chag tsel lo
De zhin sheg pa *kün ne nang wa kö pe pel* la chag tsel lo
De zhin sheg pa *rin chen pe me nam par nön pa* la chag tsel lo
De zhin sheg pa *dra chom pa yang dag par dzog pe sang gye rin po che dang pe ma la rab tu zhug pa ri wang gi gyel po* la chag tsel lo

De dag la sog pa – chog chü jig ten gyi kam tam che na – de zhin sheg pa dra chom pa yang dag par dzog pe sang gye chom den de gang ji nye chig zhug te – tso zhing zhe pe sang gye chom den de de dag tam che – dag la gong su söl

Dag gi kye wa di dang – kye wa tog me ta ma ma chi pa ne – kor wa na kor we kye ne tam che du – dig pe le gyi pa dang – gyi du tzel wa dang – gyi pa la je su yi rang wam – chö ten gyi kor ram – gen dün gyi kor ram – chog chü gen dün gyi kor trog pa dang – trog tu chug pa dang – trog pa la je su yi rang wam – tsam ma chi pa nge le gyi pa dang – gyi du tzel wa dang – gyi pa la je su yi rang wam – mi ge wa chü le kyi lam yang dag par lang wa la zhug pa dang – jug tu tzel wa dang – jug pa la je su yi rang wam – le kyi drib pa gang gi drib ne dag sem chen nyel war chi wam – dü drö kye ne su chi wam – yi dag kyi yül du chi wam – yül ta kob tu kye wam – la lor kye wam – hla tse ring po nam su kye wam – wang po ma tsang war gyur wam – ta wa log par dzin par gyur wam – sang gye jung wa la nye par mi gyi par gyur we le kyi drib pa gang lag pa de dag tam che – sang gye chom den de

ye she su gyur pa – chen du gyur pa – pang du gyur pa – tse mar gyur pa –
kyen pe zig pa – de dag gi chen ngar töl lo – chag so – mi chab bo – mi be
do – len che kyang chö ching dom par gyi lag so

Sang gye chom den de de dag tam che dag la gong su söl – dag gi kye wa di
dang – kye wa tog me ta ma ma chi pa ne – kor wa na kor we kye ne zhen
dag tu – jin pa ta na dü drö kye ne su kye pa la ze kam chig tzam tzel we ge
we tza wa gang lag pa dang – dag gi tsül trim sung pe ge we tza wa gang lag
pa dang – dag gi tsang par chö pe ge we tza wa gang lag pa dang – dag gi
sem chen yong su min par gyi pe ge we tza wa gang lag pa dang – dag gi jang
chub chog tu sem kye pe ge we tza wa gang lag pa dang – dag gi la na me pe
ye she kyi ge we tza wa gang lag pa – de dag tam che chig tu dü shing dum
te dom ne – la na ma chi pa dang – gong na ma chi pa dang – gong me yang
gong ma – la me yang la mar yong su ngo we – la na me pa yang dag par
dzog pe jang chub tu yong su ngo war gyi o

Ji tar de pe sang gye chom den de nam kyi yong su ngö pa dang – ji tar ma
jön pe sang gye chom den de nam kyi yong su ngo war gyur wa dang – ji
tar da tar zhug pe sang gye chom den de nam kyi yong su ngo war dze pa –
de zhin du dag gi kyang yong su ngo war gyi o

Dig pa tam che ni so sor shag so – sö nam tam che la ni je su yi rang ngo –
sang gye tam che la ni kül zhing söl wa deb so – dag gi la na me pe ye she
kyi chog dam pa tob par gyur chig

Mi chog gyel wa gang dag da tar zhug pa dang – gang dag de pa dag dang
de zhin gang ma jön – yön ten ngag pa ta ye gya tso dra kun la – tel mo jar
war gyi te – kyab su nye war chi o

4

Sanskrit Names of the Thirty-five Tathāgatas

The English translation of the tathāgatas' names can be replaced with the names in their original Sanskrit.

1. Shākyamuni Tathāgata Arhat Samyaksaṁ-buddha
2. Vajra-garbha-pramardin
3. Ratnārcis
4. Nāgeshvara-rāja
5. Vīrasena
6. Vīra-nandin
7. Ratnāgni
8. Ratna-chandra-prabha
9. Amogha-darshin
10. Ratna-chandra
11. Nirmala (or Vimala)
12. Shūradatta
13. Brahmā
14. Brahma-datta
15. Varuṇa
16. Varuṇa-deva
17. Bhadra-shrī
18. Chandana-shrī
19. Anantaujas
20. Prabhāsa-shrī
21. Ashoka-shrī
22. Nārāyaṇa
23. Kusuma-shrī
24. Brahma-jyotir-vikrīḍitābhijña

25. Padma-jyotir-vikrīḍitābhijña
26. Dhana-shrī
27. Smṛti-shrī
28. Suparikīrtita-nāmadheya-shrī
29. Indra-ketu-dhvaja-rāja
30. Suvikrānta-shrī
31. Yuddhajaya (or Vijita-saṃgrāma)
32. Vikrānta-gāmin-shrī
33. Samantāvabhāsa-vyūha-shrī
34. Ratna-padma-vikrāmin
35. Ratna-padma-supratiṣhṭhita-shailendra-rāja Tathāgata Arhat Samyaksaṁ-buddha.

5

The Tibetan Text:
The Bodhisattva's Confession of Downfalls

༄༅། །ཁྱུང་བ་ཆགས་དང་། སྲི་བ་ཆགས། གཙོ་རྒྱལ་མ། བཟང་སྤྱོད། བྱམས་ སྨོན། སྤྱོད་འཇུག །ཐོག་མཐའ་ མ། བདེ་སྨོན། རྗེ་སྒྲུང་ མ་སོ་གསུ་བཅུ་གསུ་ སོ།།

───────

ཀཿ ན་མོ། བྱ་ད་ཆུབ་སེམས་དཔའི་སྤྱུང་ བ་བཤགས་པ། བདག་མིང་འདི་ཞེས་⋯ བགྱིས་བ། རྡོ་རྗེ་ག་ཏུ་སྣ་མ་ལ་སྐྱབས་སུ་⋯ མཆིའོ། །སངས་རྒྱས་ལ་སྐྱབས་སུ་མཆིའོ། ཆོས་ལ་སྐྱབས་སུ་མཆིའོ། །དགེ་འདུན་ལ་⋯ སྐྱབས་སུ་མཆིའོ། །སྡོན་པ་བཙོམ་ལྡན་ འདས་དེ་བཞིན་ག་ཤེགས་པ་དགྲ་བཙོ་མ་པ་ཡང་ དག་པར་རྫོགས་པའི་སངས་རྒྱས་དཔལ་ལ་རྒྱལ་ བ་ཤྱྲྱུ་སྒྲུབ་པ་ལ་ཕྱག་འཚལ་ལོ། །དེ་བཞིན་ གཤེགས་པ་རྗེ་རྗེ་སྤྱིང་པོས་རབ་ཏུ་འཇོམས་⋯

པ་ལ་ཕྱག་འཚལ་ལོ། །དེ་བཞིན་གཤེགས་པ་
རིན་ཆེན་འོད་འཕྲོ་ལ༔། །དེ་བཞིན་གཤེགས་
པ་གྲུ་དབང་གི་རྒྱལ་པོ་ལ༔། །དེ་བཞིན་གཤེད་
པ་དཔལ་འབོའི་སྐུ་ལ༔། །དེ་བཞིན་གཤེགས་
པ་དཔལ་དགྱེས་ལ༔། །དེ་བཞིན་གཤེགས་པ་
རིན་ཆེན་མེ་ལ༔། །དེ་བཞིན་གཤེགས་པ་རིན་
ཆེན་ཟླ་འོད་ལ༔། །དེ་བཞིན་གཤེགས་པ …
མཐོང་བ་དོན་ཡོད་ལ༔། །དེ་བཞིན་གཤེགས་
པ་རིན་ཆེན་ཟླ་བ་ལ༔། །དེ་བཞིན་གཤེགས་པ་
དྲི་མ་མེད་པ་ལ༔། །དེ་བཞིན་གཤེགས་པ་
དཔལ་སྦྱིན་ལ༔། །དེ་བཞིན་གཤེགས་པ …
ཚངས་པ་ལ༔། །དེ་བཞིན་གཤེགས་པ་ཚངྒྱི
པས་བྱིན་ལ༔། །དེ་བཞིན་གཤེགས་པ་ཆུ་ལྷ་ལ༔། །དེ་བཞིན
གཤེད་པ་ཆུ་ལྷའི་ལྷ་ལ༔། །དེ་བཞིན་གཤེགས་པ་དཔལ་བཟང་
ལ༔། །དེ་བཞིན་གཤེགས་པ་ཙན་དན་དཔལ་
ལ༔། །དེ་བཞིན་གཤེགས་པ་གཟི་བརྗིད …
མཐའ་ཡས་ལ༔། །དེ་བཞིན་གཤེགས་པ …

འོད་དཔལ་ལ་×། །དེ་བཞིན་གཤེགས་པ་མྱ་
ངན་མེད་པའི་དཔལ་ལ་×། །དེ་བཞིན་གཤེགས་
པ་སྲེད་མེད་ཀྱི་བུ་ལ་×། །དེ་བཞིན་གཤེགས་
པ་མེ་ཏོག་དཔལ་ལ་×། །དེ་བཞིན་གཤེགས་
པ་ཚངས་པའི་འོད་ཟེར་རྣམ་པར་རོལ་པས་
མངོན་པར་མཁྱེན་པ་ལ་×། །དེ་བཞིན་གཤེགས་
པ་པདྨའི་འོད་ཟེར་རྣམ་པར་རོལ་པས་མངོན་
པར་མཁྱེན་པ་ལ་×། །དེ་བཞིན་གཤེགས་པ་
ནོར་དཔལ་ལ་×། །དེ་བཞིན་གཤེགས་པ་
དྲན་པའི་དཔལ་ལ་×། །དེ་བཞིན་གཤེགས་
པ་མཚན་དཔལ་ཤིན་ཏུ་ཡོངས་གྲགས་ལ་×། །
དེ་བཞིན་གཤེགས་པ་དབང་པོའི་ཏོག་གི་
རྒྱལ་མཚན་གྱི་རྒྱལ་པོ་ལ་×། །དེ་བཞིན་
གཤེགས་པ་ཤིན་ཏུ་རྣམ་པར་གནོན་པའི་
དཔལ་ལ་×། །དེ་བཞིན་གཤེགས་པ་གཡུལ་
ལས་ཤིན་ཏུ་རྣམ་པར་རྒྱལ་བ་ལ་×། །དེ་
བཞིན་གཤེགས་པ་རྣམ་པར་གནོན་པའི་

ག་ཤེགས་པ་འི་དཔལ་ལ་ལ་x། །དེ་བཞིན་
ག་ཤེགས་པ་ཀུན་ནས་སྣང་བ་བཀོད་པ་འི་
དཔལ་ལ་x། །དེ་བཞིན་ག་ཤེགས་པ་འི་
ཆེ་ནུ་པ་ཏུ་འི་རྣ་མ་པར་གནོན་པ་ལ་x། །དེ་
བཞིན་ག་ཤེགས་པ་དགྲ་བཅོམ་པ་ཡང་དག་
པར་རྫོགས་པ་འི་སངས་རྒྱས་རིན་པོ་ཆེ་དང་
པདྨ་ལ་རབ་ཏུ་བཞུ་གས་པ་རི་དབང་གི་རྒྱ་ལ་
པོ་ལ་ཕྱག་འཚལ་ལོ། །དེ་དག་ལ་སོ་གས
པ་ཕྱོ་གས་བཅུ་འི་འ་ཇིག་རྟེ་ན་གྱི་ཁམས་ཐ
ན་དེ་བཞིན་ག་ཤེགས་པ་དགྲ་བཅོམ་པ····
ཡང་དག་པར་རྫོགས་པ་འི་སངས་རྒྱས····
བཅོམ་ལྡན་འདས་གང་རྗེ་སྐྱེད་ཅིག་བཞུ་གྲ
ཏེ་འཚོ་ཞིང་གཤེས་པ་འི་སངས་རྒྱས་བཅོམ
ལྡན་འདས་དེ་དག་ཐམས་ཅད་བདག་ལ····
དགོངས་སུ་གསོ་ལ། བདག་གིས་སྐྱེ····
བ་འདི་དང་། སྐྱེ་བ་ཐོག་མའི་ཐ་མ་མེ་····
མ་ཆིས་པ་ནས་འཁོར་བ་ན་འཁོར་བའི་སྐྱེ

གནས་ཐམས་ཅད་དུ་སྤྱི་བ་ཡི་ལས་བགྱིས་
པ་དང་། བགྱིད་དུ་བསྩལ་བ་དང་། བགྱིད་
པ་ལ་རྗེས་སུ་ཡི་རང་བའམ། མཆོད་རྟེན་གྱི་
དཀོར་རམ། དགེ་འདུན་གྱི་དཀོར་རམ། ཕྱོགས་
བཅུའི་དགེ་འདུན་གྱི་དཀོར་ཕྲོགས་པ་དང་།
འཕྲོག་ཏུ་བཅུག་པ་དང་། འཕྲོག་པ་ལ་རྗེས་
སུ་ཡི་རང་བའམ། མཚམས་མ་མཆིས་པ་
ལྔའི་ལས་བགྱིས་པ་དང་། བགྱིད་དུ་བསྩལ་
བ་དང་། བགྱིད་པ་ལ་རྗེས་སུ་ཡི་རང་བའམ།
མི་དགེ་བ་བཅུའི་ལས་ཀྱི་ལམ་ཡང་དག་པར་
བླང་བ་ལ་ཞུགས་པ་དང་། འཇུག་ཏུ་བསྩལ་
བ་དང་། ཞུགས་པ་ལ་རྗེས་སུ་ཡི་རང་བ་
འམ། ལས་ཀྱི་སྒྲིབ་པ་གང་གིས་བསྒྲིབས་
ནས་བདག་སེམས་ཅན་དམྱལ་བར་མཆི་བའམ།
དུད་འགྲོའི་སྐྱེ་གནས་ལ་སུ་མཆི་བའམ། ཡི་
དགས་ཀྱི་ཡུལ་དུ་མཆི་བའམ། ཡུལ་མཐའ་
འཁོབ་ཏུ་སྐྱེ་བའམ། ཀླ་ཀློར་སྐྱེ་བའམ།

ཀླུ་ཆོ་རི་པོ་ནུམས་སུ་སྐྱེ་བའམ། དབང་པོ་མ་...
ཆང་བར་འགྱུར་བའམ། སླུ་བ་ལོག་པར་འཛིན་
པར་འགྱུར་བའམ། སངས་རྒྱས་འབྱུང་བ་ལ་
མ་ཉེས་པར་མི་བགྱིད་པར་འགྱུར་བའི་ལས་ཀྱི་...
སྒྲིབ་པ་གང་ལགས་པ་དེ་དག་ཐམས་ཅད་སངས་
རྒྱས་བཅོམ་ལྡན་འདས་ཡེ་ཤེས་སུ་གྱུར་པ།
སྤྲུན་དུ་གྱུར་པ། དབང་དུ་གྱུར་པ། ཆད་མར་
གྱུར་པ། མ་ཆེན་པས་བཟིགས་པ་དེ་དག་གི་...
སྤྱན་སྔར་མཐོལ་ལོ། །འཆགས་སོ། །མི་
འཆབ་བོ། །མི་སྦེད་དོ། །སླན་ཆད་ཀྱང་...
གཙོད་ཅིང་སྡོམ་པར་བགྱིད་ལགས་སོ། །
སངས་རྒྱས་བཅོམ་ལྡན་འདས་སྤྲུན་འདས་དེ་དག་ཐམས་
ཅད་བདག་ལ་དགོངས་སུ་གསོལ། བདག་གིས
སྐྱེ་བ་འདི་དང་། སྐྱེ་བ་ཐོག་མ་འཛི་ཐ་མ་...
མ་ཆིས་པ་ནས་འཁོར་བན་འཁོར་བ་འི་སྐྱེ་...
གནས་གཞན་དག་ཏུ་སྐྱིན་པ་ཐ་ན་དུད་འགྲོ་འི་སྐྱེ་
གནས་སུ་སྐྱེས་པ་ལ་ཟས་ཁམ་གཅི་གཙོ་མ་...

སྤྱ་ལ་བའི་དགེ་བའི་རྩ་བ་གང་ལགས་པ་དང་།

བདག་གིས་ཚུལ་ཁྲིམས་བསྲུངས་པའི་དགེ་བའི་

རྩ་བ་གང་ལགས་པ་དང་།   བདག་གིས་ཚངས་

པར་སྤྱོད་པའི་དགེ་བའི་རྩ་བ་གང་ལགས་པ་དང་།

བདག་གིས་སེམས་ཅན་ཡོངས་སུ་སྨིན་པར་···

བགྱིས་པའི་དགེ་བའི་རྩ་བ་གང་ལགས་པ་དང་།

བདག་གིས་བྱང་ཆུབ་མཆོག་ཏུ་སེམས་བསྐྱེད་

པའི་དགེ་བའི་རྩ་བ་གང་ལགས་པ་དང་། བདག

གིས་བླ་ན་མེད་པའི་ཡེ་ཤེས་ཀྱི་དགེ་བའི་རྩ་བ་

གང་ལགས་པ་དེ་དག་ཐམས་ཅད་གཅིག་གཅུ···

བསྡུས་ཤིང་བ་ཟླུམས་ཏེ་བསྡོམས་ནས་བྱུན···

མ་མཆིས་པ་དང་།   གོང་ན་མ་མཆིས་པ་དང་།

གོང་མའི་ཡང་གོང་མ། བླ་མའི་ཡང་བླ་མར་

ཡོངས་སུ་བསྔོ་བས་བླ་ན་མེད་པ་ཡང་དག་པར་

རྫོགས་པའི་བྱང་ཆུབ་ཏུ་ཡོངས་སུ་བསྔོ་བར···

བགྱིའོ། །རྗེ་ལྔར་འདས་པའི་སངས་རྒྱས···

བཙོམ་ལྡན་འདས་རྣམས་ཀྱིས་ཡོངས་སུ་བསྔོ

པ་དང་། རྗེ་སྤྱར་མ་བྱིན་པའི་སངས་རྒྱས་····
བཙོ་མ་ལྷུན་འདས་རྣམས་ཀྱིས་ཨོངས་སུ་བསྒོ་
བར་འགྱུར་བ་དང་། རྗེ་སྤྱ་རད་སྤྱར་བཅུ་ང་ས་
པའི་སངས་རྒྱས་བཙོ་མ་ལྷུན་འདས་རྣམས་ཀྱིས་
ཨོ་ངས་སུ་བསྒོ་བར་མཛད་པ་དེ་བཞིན་དུ་བདག་
གིས་ཀྱང་ཨོངས་སུ་བསྒོ་བར་བགྱིའོ། །སྡིག་
པ་ཐམས་ཅད་ནི་སོ་སོར་འཆགས་སོ། །བསོད་
ནམས་ཐམས་ཅད་ཅད་ལ་ནི་རྗེས་སུ་ཡི་རང་ངོ་། །
སངས་རྒྱས་ཐམས་ཅད་ལ་ནི་བསྐུལ་ཞིང་གསོལ་
བ་འདེབས་སོ། །བདག་གིས་བྷན་མེད་པའི་
ཡེ་ཤེས་ཀྱི་མཆོག་དམ་པ་ཐོབ་པར་གྱུར་ཅིག །
མི་མཆོག་རྒྱལ་བ་གང་དག་དང་སྤྱར་བཞུགས་པ་
དང་། །གང་དག་འདས་པ་དག་དང་དེ་བཞིན····
གང་མ་བྱོན། །ཨོན་ཏན་བསྔ་གས་པ་མཐའ····
ཡས་རྒྱ་མཚོ་འད་ཀུན་ལ། །ཐལ་མོ་སྦྱར་བར····
བགྱིས་ཏེ་སྐྱབས་སུ་ཉེ་བར་མཆིའོ། །ཨཿགས་པ····
རང་པོ་གསུམ་པ་ཞེ་ས་བྱ་བ་ཐེག་པ་ཆེན་པོའི་མདོ་རྟོགས་སོ།། ||

6

Outline of A Significant Sight: A Commentary to the Bodhisattva's Confession of Downfalls

(Many of the outline headings found here have been abbreviated in the translation, several have been modified, and IC2a and IC2b have been omitted altogether.)

I.   How to confess negativities and downfalls
IA. How to confess negativities and downfalls by means of showing
     the force of the basis
IB. How to confess negativities and downfalls by means of showing
     the force of applying all antidotes
IC. How to confess negativities and downfalls by means of showing
     the force of total repudiation
  IC1.   Request to witness the confession of negativities and downfalls
  IC2.   Identifying the negativities and obscurations to be confessed
    IC2a.   Shown in brief
    IC2b.   Explained extensively
      IC2b-1.   Explaining the negativities of misusing the possessions of
          the Jewels
      IC2b-2.   Explaining the negativities of the five [actions of]
          immediate [retribution]
      IC2b-3.   Explaining the negativities included in the ten non-virtues
  IC3.   How to confess those negativities and downfalls
ID. How to confess negativities and downfalls by means of showing
     the force of turning away from faults in the future

II.   How to dedicate virtues
IIA.   Request to witness the dedication
IIB.   Identifying the virtues to be dedicated
IIC.   How to dedicate

III.   Summarizing the meaning, showing the seven limbs in their entirety
IIIA. Explaining the manner in which there are seven limbs
IIIB. For the purpose of showing the seven limbs, again showing how
        to go for refuge to the Three Jewels

7

How to Perform Full-length Prostrations

(1) Put the palms of your hands together with the thumbs aligned and tucked into the center of your palms. Your folded thumbs represent offering a wish-fulfilling jewel to the buddhas.

Note: Having visualized the thirty-five buddhas in the space before you, imagine that you emanate countless bodies, each of which has many heads with many tongues. As you prostrate, imagine that all the emanated bodies, visualized surrounding you, do the same.

(2) Place your folded hands upon the crown of your head. This creates the cause to obtain the crown protuberance (*ushnisha*) of a buddha.

Note: Simultaneously recite the phrase of prostration to the corresponding tathāgata while imagining that each of the emanated tongues also does the same. Continue to repeat that same phrase of prostration until the prostration is complete.

(3) Touch your folded hands to your forehead (optional). This purifies negative actions committed by the body and creates the cause to obtain the treasure hair of a buddha.

Note: If you prefer to do prostrations without touching your hands to your forehead, visualize that touching your crown purifies negative actions committed by the body.

(4) Touch your folded hands to your neck. This purifies negative actions committed by speech and creates the cause to obtain the melodious speech of a buddha with its sixty-four qualities.

(5) Touch your folded hands to your heart. This purifies negative actions committed by mind and creates the cause to obtain the qualities of a buddha's mind, such as the twenty-one divisions of uncontaminated exalted wisdom.

Note: While touching your hands to the forehead (or crown), neck, and heart visualize that white light and nectar radiate from the corresponding place of the body of the buddha to whom you are prostrating and enter, respectively, into your own forehead, neck, and heart, completely purifying all your negativities of body, speech, and mind. If you find this visualization difficult, merely visualize that white light and nectar radiate from the heart of the buddha to whom you are prostrating, enter into your body through your forehead, and purify all your negativities of body, speech, and mind. Visualize that all your negativities leave your body through your lower orifices in the form of filthy dirt, snakes, scorpions, and so forth. These fall into the gaping mouth of the Lord of Death, who is visualized seven levels under the ground below your feet. The Lord of Death becomes extremely blissful and satisfied.

(6) Bend forward and place your hands flat on the ground with your fingers very slightly apart.

(7) Lower your knees and stretch your body out full-length on the ground with your arms extended forward.

Note: It is said that the amount of negative actions purified by a single prostration is in proportion to the number of atoms of earth covered by the extended body; therefore, also visualize that your body is extremely huge and covers an enormous amount of earth.

(8) Either (a) lift merely your palms up off the ground or (b) bend your elbows and bring your folded hands over the back of your head; then lower your palms once again to the ground.

Note: While doing this, visualize that a replica of the buddha to whom you are prostrating absorbs into you, thereby, blessing you.

(9) To stand up bring your hands back to shoulder level, raise up on your knees, place your hands on the ground close to the level of your knees, raise your knees off the ground, then raise your hands, and stand up straight.

(10) Begin the next prostration by immediately placing your folded hands on the crown of your head.

Note: At the end of the final prostration once again touch your folded hands to the crown, forehead (optional), neck, and heart. Visualize that your body is completely pure and transparent, like clear crystal, and feel convinced that all your negative actions of body, speech, and mind have been completely purified.

How to Perform Short Prostrations

(1) Touch your folded hands, with thumbs tucked inside the palms, to your crown, forehead (optional), neck, and heart as above.

(2) Bend forward, place your hands flat upon the ground, lower your knees to the ground, and touch your forehead to the ground.

Note: Five points of the body should always touch the ground—the hands, knees, and head.

(3) When standing up, first the head leaves the ground, then the knees, and finally the hands.

Note: You should come to a straight standing position before beginning the next prostration.

(4) Begin the next prostration by immediately placing your folded hands on the crown of your head.

Note: At the end of the final prostration once again touch your folded hands to the crown, forehead (optional), neck, and heart. Short prostrations are generally performed at the beginning and end of Dharma teachings, during the Restoring and Purifying Ceremony of monks and nuns, etc.

How to Perform Very Simple Prostrations

(1) Hold your folded hands, with thumbs tucked inside your palms, at your heart.

Note: The practice of confession to the thirty-five buddhas is usually accompanied by full-length prostrations but can be done with either the short or very simple prostrations when space or health do not permit full-length prostrations.

Notes

1. For a complete version see Janice D. Willis's *Enlightened Beings*.

2. The five lay vows are the vows taken by lay Dharma practitioners to abandon killing, stealing, sexual misconduct, lying, and taking intoxicants.

3. Dakas and dakinis are, respectively, male and female Dharma practitioners who have the appearance of gods. There are three types: (1) the mantra born (*sngags skyes*), who are practitioners of the generation stage of tantra; (2) the simultaneously born (*lhan skyes*), who are practitioners of the completion stage of tantra; and (3) the field born (*zhing skyes*), who are born in a special place, such as one of the twenty-four holy places of Heruka.

4. Supermundane Dharma protectors are wrathful emanations of buddhas who eliminate hindrances to our Dharma practice. Mundane Dharma protectors are worldly beings who have pledged to protect the Dharma and the beings who practice it.

5. A superior is a being who has directly realized emptiness, the ultimate mode of existence of all phenomena. The exalted wisdom realizing emptiness cuts through the ignorance grasping at an inherently existent self of persons and self of phenomena, the source of all other mental afflictions.

6. The syllable *man* of *mantra* means "mind," while *tra* means "to protect." Therefore, a mantra is that which protects the mind. According to the sutra teachings, mantras protect the mind from the afflictions, while according to the tantra teachings, mantras protect the mind from ordinary appearances and grasping at ordinary appearances.

7. A stupa is a Buddhist reliquary monument representing the omniscient mind of a buddha. It contains relics—whether of a highly realized being or an ordinary person—that have been purified and consecrated by particular rituals and thereby transformed into objects worthy of veneration.

8. For an explanation of the four results in relation to each of the ten non-virtuous paths of actions see *An Anthology of Well-Spoken Advice*, pp. 339–342; *Liberation in Our Hands*, part 2, pp. 256–257; and *Liberation in the Palm of Your Hand*, pp. 452–453.

9. For an extensive explanation of the qualities of a buddha's four bodies see Haribhadra's *Clear Meaning Commentary and Liberation in Our Hands*, part 2, appendix E.

10. For an extensive explanation of the thirty-two major marks see *An Anthology of Well-Spoken Advice*, pp. 243–249, and for an explanation of both the major and minor marks see *Liberation in Our Hands*, part 2, appendix E, pp. 308–314.

11. For an extensive explanation of the qualities of a buddha's speech see *The Sixty Branches of Melodious Speech* included in Chandrakīrti's *Supplement to (Nāgārjuna's) "Treatise on the Middle Way,"* translated by T. Jampa and G. Churinoff; and lam-rim texts such as *An Anthology of Well-Spoken Advice*, pp. 251–257, and *Liberation in Our Hands*, part 2, appendix E, pp. 315–320.

12. For an extensive explanation of the qualities of a buddha's mind see *An Anthology of Well-Spoken Advice*, pp. 258–262; and *Liberation in Our Hands*, part 2, appendix E, pp. 294–307.

13. For a detailed discussion of the meditation on the seven, the six causes and one effect, see lam-rim texts such as *Liberation in the Palm of Your Hand*, pp. 566–587.

14. Nirvana, or liberation, is the state achieved when the afflictions and their seeds are completely eliminated from the mental continuum. The foe-destroyers who have achieved nirvana have reached a state of personal peace but, unlike the buddhas, they do not work to free all sentient beings from suffering.

15. It seems likely that a change in the Tibetan text has occurred since the original Sanskrit word *vīra* (meaning hero, brave, courageous, etc.), which would have been correctly translated into Tibetan as *dpa'* (also meaning hero, brave, courageous, etc.), here, however, appears as *dpal* (glorious). Probably over time the Tibetan *a* was changed to *la*. It has been translated here in accordance with the original Sanskrit.

16. Here again the Tibetan *dpa'* (hero, brave, courageous, etc.) seems to have been changed to *dpal* (glorious), since the Sanskrit *shūra* (as does

vīra) means hero, brave, courageous, etc. Again here it has been translated in accordance with the original Sanskrit.

17. The five actions of immediate retribution are also called the five heinous
crimes, the five extreme negative actions, and the five immediate karmas.

18. For a detailed discussion of the root and secondary afflictions see
Meditation on Emptiness, pp. 255–266.

19. For an explanation of the first four wisdoms see *Liberation in Our
Hands,* part 2, appendix E, pp. 291–293. The fifth, the wisdom of the
completely pure sphere of phenomena, although called a wisdom, actually refers to the nature body of a buddha. However, generally speaking
it can be said to mean the wisdom realizing emptiness.

20. Root text (*gzhung*) refers to the actual *Sutra of the Bodhisattva's
Confession of Downfalls.*

21. Cast-Afar is a synonym of Hedonist (*charvaka, tshu rol mdzes pa*). The
followers of this particular philosophical school, which existed in India at
the time of Buddha, are so-called because they are considered by the
Buddhist schools to have cast afar, or to have rejected, the correct view
concerning the law of actions and results, past and future lives, and so on.

22. The actual meaning of dharani (retention) is recollection and wisdom.
A mantra-dharani, or dharani of mantra, is a mantra that brings about
the development of recollection and wisdom by enabling us to retain,
or to hold, words and their meanings in our mind. Therefore, this is a
case of giving the name of the result to its cause.

Glossary

English	Sanskrit	Tibetan
action	karma	las
action tantra	kriyātantra	bya rgyud
affliction	klesha	nyon mongs
afflictive obscuration	kleshāvaraṇa	nyon mong pa'i sgrib pa
aggregate/heap	skandha	phung po
anger	pratigha	khong khro
animal	tiryagyoni	dud 'gro
antidote/opponent	pratipakṣha	gnyen po
attachment	rāga	'dod chags
attainment	siddhi	dngos grub
auspiciousness	pratītyasamutpāda	rten 'brel
barbarian	turuṣhka	kla klo
basis	ādhāra/vastu	gzhi
benefit	anushamṣha	phan yon
bodhisattva	bodhisattva	byang chub sems dpa'
border area	prānta	yul mtha' khob
branch	aṅga	yan lag
buddha	buddha	sangs rgyas
Cast-Afar	ayata	rbyang phan pa
cause	hetu	rgyu
collections of doctrine	dharmaskandha	chos kyi phung po
commitment	samāya	dam tshigs
compassion	karuṇā	snying rje
completion	—	mthar thug
compositional factor	saṃskāra	'du byed

concealment	mrakṣha	'chab pa
concentration	dhyāna	bsam gtan
confession	deshana	bshags pa
conqueror	jina	rgyal ba
consciousness	vijñāna	rnam par shes pa
constituent	dhātu	khams
conventional truth	saṃvṛtisatya	kun rdzob bden pa
covetousness	abhidhyā	brnab sems
cyclic existence	saṃsāra	'khor ba
daka/dakini	ḍāka/ḍākiṇī	mkha' 'gro (ma)
dedication	pariṇāma	bsngo ba
definite goodness	niḥshreyasa	nges legs
demon	māra	bdud
dependent relation	pratītyasamutpāda	rten 'brel
desire realm	kāmadhātu	'dod khams
Dharma	dharma	chos
Dharma protector	dharmapāla	chos skyong
direct perception/perceiver	pratyakṣha	mngon sum
disciple	vineya	gdul bya
discipline	vinaya	'dul ba
discordant class	vipakṣha	mi mthun pa'i phyogs
discrimination	saṃjñā	'du shes
divisive speech	paishunya	phra mar smra ba
doctrine	dharma	chos
doubt	vichikitsā	the tshom
downfall	āpatti	ltung ba
emanation body	nirmāṇakāya	sprul sku
emptiness	shūnyatā	stong pa nyid
enemy/foe	ari	dgra
enjoyment body	saṃbhogakāya	longs sku
enlightenment	bodhi	byang chub
environmental result	ādhipatiphala	bdag po'i 'bras bu
eon	kalpa	bskal pa
equanimity	upekṣhā	btang snyoms

exalted wisdom	jñāna	ye shes
execution/preparation	prayoga	sbyor ba
faith	shraddhā	dad pa
feeling	vedanā	tshor ba
foe-destroyer	arhat/arhan	dgra bcom pa
force of applying all antidotes	—	gnyen po kun tu spyod pa'i stobs
force of the basis	—	rten gyi stobs
force of total repudiation	—	rnam par sun 'byin pa'i stobs
force of turning away from faults in the future	—	nye pa las slar ldog pa'i stobs
form	rūpa	gzugs
form body	rūpakāya	gzugs sku
form realm	rūpadhātu	gzugs khams
formless realm	ārūpyadhātu	gzugs med khams
formulated misdeed	pratikṣhepaṇa-sāvadya	bcas pa'i kha na ma tho ba
fully ordained monk	bhikṣhu	dge slong
fully ordained nun	bhikṣhunī	dge slong ma
generosity	dāna	sbyin pa
god	deva	hla
Great Vehicle	mahāyāna	theg pa chen po
ground	bhūmi	sa
happiness	sukha	bde ba
harsh words	pāruṣhya	tshig rtsub smra ba
hatred	dveṣha	zhe sdang
heap/aggregate	skandha	phung po
hearer	shrāvaka	nyan thos
Hedonist	chārvāka	tshu rol mdzes pa
hell	naraka	dmyal ba
high status	abhyudaya	mngon mtho
highest yoga tantra	anuttarayogatantra	rnal 'byor bla med rgyud

homage	nāmo	'dud pa
human	manushya	mi
hungry ghost	preta	yi dvags
idle talk	pralapa	ngag 'khyal
ignorance	avidyā/moha	ma rig pa/gti mug
immeasurable	apramāna	tshad med
immediate [retribution]	ānantarya	mtshams med pa
imprint	vāsanā	bags chags
introspection	samprajanya	shes bzhin
jealousy	īrshyā	phrag dog
Jewel	ratna	dkon mchog
joyous effort	vīrya	brtson 'grus
karmic obscuration	karmāvarana	las kyi sgrib pa
killing	prānātighāta	srog gcod
lay vows	upāsaka/upāsikā	dge bsnyen
leisureless	akshana	mi khom pa
Lesser Vehicle	hīnayāna	theg dman
liberation	moksha	thar pa
limb	anga	yan lag
love	maitri	byams pa
lying	mrshāvāda	rdzun du smra ba
major mark	nimitta	mtshan bzang
malice	vyāpāda	gnod sems
maturation result	vipākaphala	rnam smin gyi 'bras bu
meaning	artha	don
meditation	bhāvanā	sgoms pa
meditative stabilization	samādhi	ting nge 'dzin
mental factor	chaitta	sems byung
mercy	anukampā/dayā	brtse ba
merit	punya	bsod nams
method	upāya	thabs

migrator/migration	gati	'gro ba
mind	chitta	sems
mind of enlightenment	bodhichitta	byang chub kyi sems
mindfulness	smṛti	dran pa
minor mark	anuvyañjana	dpe byad
morality	shīla	tshul khrims
motivation	samutthāna	kun nas slong ba
natural misdeed	prakṛti-sāvadya	rang bzhin gyi kha na ma tho ba
nature body	svabhāvikakāya	ngo bo nyid sku
negative action	pāpakarma	sdig pa'i las
negativity	pāpa	sdig pa
nirvana	nirvāṇa	mya ngan las 'das pa
non-associated compositional factor	viprayukta-saṃskāra	ldan min 'du byed
non-virtue	akushala	mi dge ba
Not Low	akaniṣṭa	'og min
novice monk	shrāmaṇera	dge tsul
object	viṣhaya	yul
object of abandonment	prahātvya (?)	spang bya
object of knowledge	jñeya	shes bya
obscuration	āvaraṇa	sgrib pa
obscuration of maturation	vipāka-āvaraṇa	rnam smin gyi sgrib pa
obscurations to omniscience/objects of knowledge	jñeyāvaraṇa	shes sbya'i grib pa
offering	pūjā	mchod pa
One Gone Thus	tathāgata	de bzhin gshegs pa
One Gone to Bliss	sugata	bde bar gshegs pa
opponent force	pratipakṣhabala	gnyen po stobs
path	mārga	lam
patience	kṣhānti	bzod pa
perfection	pāramitā	pha rol tu phyin pa

perfectly complete	samyaksaṃ	yang dag par rdzogs pa
performance tantra	charyātantra	spyod rgyud
person/being	pudgala/puruṣha	gang zag/skyes bu
phenomenon	dharma	chos
poison	viṣha	dug
pride	māna	nga rgyal
prostration	abhivandana	phyag 'tshal
pure conduct	brahmacharyā	tshangs spyod
quality	guṇa	yon tan
realm	dhātu	khams
recognition	saṃjñā	'du shes
refuge	sharaṇa	skyabs
regret	kaukṛtya	'gyod pa
rejoice	anumodana	rjes su yid rang ba
respect/devout	ādara/bhakti	gus pa
result	phala	'bras bu
result corresponding to the cause	niṣhyandaphala	rgyu mthun gyi 'bras bu
(1) as an activity	—	byed pa rgyu mthun gyi 'bras bu
(2) as an experience	—	myong ba rgyu mthun gyi 'bras bu
retention	dhāraṇī	gzungs
root of virtue	kushala-mūla	dge ba'i rtsa ba
root text	grantha	gzhung
sangha	saṅgha	dge 'dun
secondary action of immediate retribution	upānantarīya	nye ba mtshams med pa
sentient being	sattva	sems can
sexual misconduct	kāmamithyācāra	'dod pas log par g.yem pa
solitary realizer	pratyekabuddha	rang sangs rgyas
son-of-the-gods	devaputra	hla'i bu
spiritual teacher	guru	bla ma

stealing	adattādāna	ma byin len
stupa	stūpa	mchod rten
Subduer	muni	thub pa
suffering	duḥkha	sdug bsngal
superior	ārya	'phags pa
sutra	sūtra	mdo
thought	chintā	bsam pa
Three Jewels	triratna	dkon mchog gsum
three poisons	triviṣha	dug gsum
thusness/suchness	tathatā	de bzhin nyid
Transcendent Endowed Destroyer	bhagavan	bcom ldan 'das
true cessations	nirodhasatya	'gog pa'i bden pa
true origins	samudayasatya	kun 'byung bden pa
true paths	mārgasatya	lam gyi bden pa
true sufferings	duḥkhasatya	sdug bsngal bden pa
truth	satya	bden pa
truth body	dharmakāya	chos sku
ultimate truth	paramārthasatya	don dam bden pa
unpredicted/neutral	avyākṛta	lung ma bstan
Unrelenting Torment	avīchi	mnar med
unsurpassed/highest	anuttara	bla na med pa
view	dṛṣhṭi	lta ba
virtue	kushala	dge ba
wisdom	prajñā	shes rab
wisdom truth body	jñānadharmakāya	ye shes chos sku
Without Discrimination	asaṃjña	'du shes med pa
world system	lokadhātu	'jig rten gyi khams
wrong view	mithyādṛṣhṭi	log par lta ba
yoga tantra	pratidesaniya	rnal 'byor rgyud

Bibliography

Note: Sutras and tantras are listed alphabetically according to their English title in the first section; Indian and Tibetan treatises are listed alphabetically according to their author in the second section; and other works are listed alphabetically according to their author in the third section. Some of the English titles have been abbreviated.

The following abbreviations have been used:

P: *The Tibetan Tripiṭaka.* Peking edition, edited by Dr. Daisetz T. Suzuki. Tokyo, Japan: Suzuki Research Foundation, 1962.

T: *A Complete Catalogue of the Tibetan Buddhist Canons.* Edited by Hakuju Ui, Munetada Suzuki, Yensho Kanakura, Tokan Tada. Sendai, Japan: Tohoku Imperial University, 1934.

1. Sutras and Tantras

Dharani That Exhorts
Chuṇḍādhāraṇī
bsKul byed kyi gzungs
(Not listed in P or T)

Guhyasamāja Tantra
Sarvatathāgatakāyavākchittarahasyaguhyasamājanāmamahākalparāja
De bzhin gshegs pa thams cad kyi sku gsung thugs kyi gsang chen gsang ba 'dus pa zhes bya ba brtag pa'i rgyal po chen po
P81 Vol. 3
Partial translation in A. Wayman's *The Yoga of the Guhyasamājatantra,* Delhi: Motilal, 1977.

Heap of Jewels Sutra
Ārya mahāratnakūṭadharmaparyāyashatasāhasrikagrantha sūtra
'Phags pa dkon mchog brtsegs pa chen po'i chos kyi rnam grangs le'u stong phrag brgya pa'i mdo
P760 Vol. 22–24

King of Prayers of Good Conduct
Ārya bhadracharyāpraṇidhānarāja
'Phags pa bzang po spyod pa'i smon lam gyi rgyal po
P716 Vol. 11; T1095

Translation by Martin Willson, *The Noble King of Vows of the Conduct of Samantabhadra,* in *Shakyamuni Puja,* Boston: Wisdom Publications, 1988.

One Hundred Actions
Karmashataka
Las brgya tham pa
P1007 Vol. 39; T340
Also known as *The Sutra of One Hundred Actions.*
Karmashatakasūtra
mDo sde las brgya pa

Sutra Indicating the Four Dharmas
Ārya chaturdharmanirdesha nāma mahāyāna sūtra
'Phags pa chos bzhi bstan pa zhes bya ba theg pa chen po'i mdo
T249

Sutra of the Bodhisattva's Confession of Downfalls
Byang chub sems dpa'i ltung ba bshags pa
(See *Sutra of the Three Heaps*)

Sutra of the Three Heaps
Ārya triskandhaka nāma mahāyāna sūtra
'Phags pa phung po gsum pa zhes bya ba theg pa chen po'i mdo
P950 Vol. 38; T284
Translations in Brian Beresford's *Mahāyāna Purification,* Dharamsala: Library of Tibetan Works and Archives, 1980; Kathleen McDonald's *How to Meditate,* Boston: Wisdom Publications, 1984, 1995; Pabongka Rinpoche's *Liberation in the Palm of Your Hand,* Boston: Wisdom Publications, 1991; and Martin Willson's *Rites and Prayers,* London: Wisdom Publications, 1985.

Sutra of the Wise and the Foolish
Damamūko nāma sūtra
mDzangs blun zhe bya ba'i mdo
P1008 Vol. 40; T341
Dharamsala: Tibetan Cultural Printing Press, 1980. Translation from the Mongolian by Stanley Frye, *Sutra of the Wise and the Foolish* (sic.) or *The Ocean of Narratives* (üliger-ün dalai), Dharamsala: Library of Tibetan Works and Archives, 1981.

Vinaya
Vinaya
'Dul ba
P1030–55 Vol.41–45; T1–7

2. SANSKRIT AND TIBETAN TREATISES

Chandrakīrti (Zla-ba-grags-pa)
Supplement to (Nāgārjuna's) 'Treatise on the Middle Way'
Madhyamakāvatāra
dbU ma la 'jug pa
P5261 Vol. 98; P5262 Vol. 98
Translated by Thubten Jampa and George Churinoff, Pomaia, Italy: Istituto Lama
Tzong Khapa, 1990, unpublished.

Gendün Drub (dGe-'dun grub) (First Dalai Lama) (1391–1474)
*Clarifying the Path to Liberation: A Complete Explanation of the Treasury of
Abhidharma*
mDzod ṭig tar lam gsal byed
Sarnath, India: The Pleasure of Elegant Sayings Printing Press, 1973. Partial
translation by David Patt (1993, unpublished thesis) and the introduction and
chapters 1 and 2 by George Churinoff, Pomaia, Italy: Istituto Lama Tzong Khapa,
1992, unpublished.

Gyeltsab (rGyal-tshab) (1364–1432)
The Benefits of the Names of the Thirty-Five Buddhas
Sangs rgyas sum cu so lnga'i mtshan gyi phan yon bzhugs
Included in *The Collected Works of Gyeltsab Dharma Rinchen* (rGyal tshab dar ma rin
chen gyi gsung 'bum), Vol. 1. New Delhi: Guru Deva, 1982.

Haribhadra (Seng-ge bzang-po)
Clear Meaning Commentary
Sphutartha
Shes rab kyi pha rol tu phyin pa'i man ngag gi bstan bcos mngon par rtogs pa'i
rgyan gyi 'grel ba don gsal
Sarnath, India: Central Institute of Higher Tibetan Studies, 1977. Translation by
Thubten Jampa and George Churinoff, Pomaia, Italy: Istituto Lama Tzong Khapa,
1985, unpublished.

Jaitāri (dGra las rgyal ba)
*Stages of Training of a Bodhisattva: A Commentary to the Bodhisattva's Confession of
Downfalls*
Bodhyāpattideshānavṛtti-bodhisattvasikṣhākramanāma
Byang chub kyi ltung ba bshags pa'i 'grel pa byang chub sems dpa'i bslab pa'i rim
pa zhes bya ba
T4006

Jetsün Chökyi Gyeltsen (rJe-btsun chos-kyi rgyal-mtshan)
The Ocean Playground of the Lord of the Nāgas
Shes rab kyi pha rol tu phyin pa'i man ngag gi bstan bcos mngon par rtogs pa'i
rgyan 'grel pa dang bcas pa'i rnam bshad rnam pa gnyis kyi dka' ba'i gnas gsal bar
byed pa legs bshad skal bzang klu dbang gi rol mtsho zhes bya ba
Xining, China: mTso sngon mi rigs par khang, 1991.

Lang-ri Tangpa Dorje Seng-ge (gLang-ri thang-pa rdo-rje seng-ges) (1054–1123)
Eight Verses on Mind Training
bLo sbyong tsig rkang brgyad ma lo rgyus dang bcad pa
Included in *Sems dpa' chen po dkon mchog rgyal mtshan gyis phyogs bsgrigs mdzad pa'i
blo sbyong brgya rtsa dang dkar chag gdung sel zla ba bcas.* Compiled by dKon
mchog rgyal mtsan. Dharamsala: Shes rig par khang, 1973.
Translation by B. Beresford, *Thought Transformation in Eight Stanzas,* in Geshe
Rabten and Geshe Dhargyey's *Advice from a Spiritual Friend,* Boston: Wisdom
Publications, 1984, 1996; and by Jeffrey Hopkins in Tenzin Gyatso, *Kindness,
Clarity and Insight,* Ithaca, N.Y.: Snow Lion Publications, 1985.

Maitreya (Byams-pa)
Sublime Continuum of the Great Vehicle
Mahāyāna-uttara-tantra-shāstra (also known as Ratna-gotra-vibhāga)
Theg pa chen po rgyud bla ma'i bstan bcos
P5525 Vol. 108; T4024
Translated by E. Obermiller, *Sublime Science of the Great Vehicle to Salvation* (Acta
Orientalia, XI, ii, iii, and iv); and by J. Takasaki, *A Study on the Ratnagotravibhāga,*
Rome: IS.M.E.O, 1966.

Nāgārjuna (kLu-sgrub)
Commentary to the Bodhisattva's Confession of Downfalls
Bodhyāpattideshanāvṛtti
Byang chub kyi ltung ba bshags pa'i 'grel pa
T4005
Translation by Brian Beresford, *The Commentary to the "Declaration of Downfalls of
an Awakening (Warrior)"* in *Mahāyāna Purification,* Dharamsala: Library of Tibetan
Works and Archives, 1980.

Friendly Letter
Suhṛllekha
bShes pa'i spring yig
P5682 Vol. 129; T4182 and 4496
Translation by Geshe L. Tharchin and A. B. Engle, *Nāgārjuna's Letter,* Dharamsala:
Library of Tibetan Works and Archives, 1979.

Panchen Lozang Chökyi Gyeltsen (Pan-chen blo-bzang chos-kyi rgyal-mtshan)
(1569–1662)
*Indivisibility of Bliss and Emptiness: A Ritual of the Profound Path of Offering to the
Guru*
Guru pūjasya kalpa nāma
Zab lam bla ma mchod pa'i cho ga bde stong dbyer med ma
Reprinted in *bLa ma'i rnal 'byor dang yi dam khag gi bdag bskyed sogs zhal 'don gces
btus,* Dharamsala: Shes rig par khang, 1979.
Translations by Dr. Alexander Berzin, *The Guru Puja,* Dharamsala: Library of
Tibetan Works and Archives, 1979; Thubten Jinpa in Tenzin Gyatso, *The Union of
Bliss and Emptiness,* Ithaca, N.Y.: Snow Lion Publications, 1988; and Martin
Willson, *A Ritual of the Profound Path of Offering to the Guru,* in *Rites and Prayers,*
London: Wisdom Publications, 1985.

Panchen Lozang Yeshe (Pan-chen blo-bzang ye-shes) (1663–1737)
Quick Path—Stages of the Path
Lam rim myur lam
Included in *The Collected Works of Panchen Lozang Yeshe*
Pan chen blo bzang ye shes kyi gsung 'bum
New Delhi: bKra shis hlun po Monastery, 1981.

Sanggye Yeshe (Sangs-rgyas ye-shes) (1525–1591)
A Significant Sight: A Commentary to the Bodhisattva's Confession of Downfalls
Byang chub sems dpa'i ltung ba bshags pa'i ṭikka don ldan ces bya ba bzhugs
Listed among *The Collected Works of Sanggye Yeshe* but mistakenly included in *The
Collected Works of Tsechogling Yongdzin Yeshe Gyeltsen* (Tshe mchog gling yongs 'dzin
ye shes rgyal mtshan gyi gsung 'bum) Vol. 14, New Delhi: Tibet House Library,
1974.

Shāntideva (Zhi-ba-hla) (c. 700)
Compendium of Instructions
Shikṣhāsamuchchayakārikā
bsLab pa kun las btus pa'i tshig le'ur byas pa
P5336 Vol. 102, T3939
Translation by C. Bendall and W.H.D. Rouse, *Śikṣa Samuccaya.* Delhi: Motilal,
1971.

Engaging in the Bodhisattva Deeds
Bodhisattvacharyāvatāra
Byang chub sems dpa'i spyod pa la 'jug pa
P5272 Vol. 99
Translation by Stephen Batchelor, *A Guide to the Bodhisattva's Way of Life,*
Dharamsala: Library of Tibetan Works and Archives, 1979.

Trijang Dorje Chang (Khri byang rdo rje 'chang) (1901–1981)
Collected Works About Mind Training
bLo sbyong gi skor sogs gsung thor bu'i rigs rnams phyogs gcig tu bsdebs pa
Included in *The Collected Works of Trijang Dorje Chang* (Yongs rdzogs bstan pa'i
mnga' bdag skyabs rje yongs 'dzin khri byang rdo rje 'chang chen po'i gsung 'bum)
Vol. *ga*, New Delhi: Guru Deva, undated.

Tsongkhapa (Tsong-kha-pa) (1357–1419)
Practice of the Thirty-five Buddhas and a Description of the Deities' Bodies
Sangs rgyas so lnga'i mngon rtogs dang hla skua'i phyag tshad
Included in *The Collected Works of Tsongkhapa* (Kham gsum chos kyi rgyal po shar
rgyal ba tsong kha pa chen po po'i gsung 'bum) Vol. 11, New Delhi: Guru Deva,
1978.

Lines of Experience (or) *The Abbreviated Meaning of the Stages of the Path*
Nyams mgur (or) Lam rim bsdus don
In *The Collected Works* (ibid.) Vol. 2, New Delhi: Guru Deva, (date?). Miscellanea
(thor bu) 55–58
Translation by Robert A. F. Thurman, *Lines of Experience,* in *The Life and Teachings
of Tsong Khapa,* Dharamsala: Library of Tibetan Works and Archives, 1982.

Vasubandhu (dbYig-gnyen) (fourth century)
Explanation of the 'Treasury of Knowledge'
Abhidharmakoshabhāṣhya
Chos mngon pa'i mdzod kyi bshad pa
P5591 Vol. 115; T4090
Translations by Louis de La Vallée Poussin, *L'Abhidharmakośa de Vasubandhu,* Paris:
Geuthner, 1923–31 and Bruxelles: Institut Belge des Hautes Etudes Chinoises,
1971; by Leo M. Pruden, *Abhidharmakośabhāṣhyam,* Berkeley: Asian Humanities
Press, 1988; and the introduction and chapter 1 by George Churinoff, Pomaia,
Italy: Istituto Lama Tzong Khapa, 1990, unpublished.

Yeshe Gyeltsen (Tse mchog gling yongs 'dzin ye shes rgyal mtsan) (1713–1793)
Biographies of the Lineage Gurus of the Stages of the Path
Lam rim bla ma brgyud pa'i rnam thar
Xining, China: mTso sngon mi rigs par 'debs bzo grva khang, 1990.

3. OTHER WORKS

Batchelor, Stephen. *A Guide to the Bodhisattva's Way of Life*. Dharamsala: Library of Tibetan Works and Archives, 1979.

Bendall, C. and Rouse, W.H.D. *Śikṣa Samuccaya*. Delhi: Motilal, 1971.

Beresford, Brian. *Mahāyāna Purification*. Dharamsala: Library of Tibetan Works and Archives, 1980.

Berzin, Alexander. *The Guru Puja*. Dharamsala: Library of Tibetan Works and Archives, 1979.

Dhargyey, Ngawang. *An Anthology of Well-Spoken Advice*. Dharamsala: Library of Tibetan Works and Archives, 1982.

Gyatso, Tenzin (bsTan-'dzin rgya-mtsho), the Dalai Lama. *Kindness, Clarity, and Insight*. Ithaca, N.Y.: Snow Lion Publications, 1985.

Gyatso, Tenzin, the Dalai Lama. *Opening the Eye of New Awareness*. Boston: Wisdom Publications, 1985.

Gyatso, Tenzin, the Dalai Lama. *The Union of Bliss and Emptiness*. Ithaca, N.Y.: Snow Lion Publications, 1988.

Hopkins, Jeffrey. *Meditation on Emptiness*. Boston: Wisdom Publications, 1983, 1996.

McDonald, Kathleen. *How to Meditate*. Boston: Wisdom Publications, 1984.

Pabongka Rinpoche (Pha-bong-kha). *Liberation in Our Hand, Parts One and Two*. Translated by Geshe Lobsang Tharchin with Artemus B. Engle. Howell, New Jersey: Mahayana Sutra and Tantra Press, 1990 and 1994.

Pabongka Rinpoche. *Liberation in the Palm of Your Hand*. Translated by Michael Richards. Boston: Wisdom Publications, 1991.

Rabten, Geshe and Dhargyey, Geshe. *Advice From a Spiritual Friend*. Boston: Wisdom Publications, 1984 and 1996.

Thurman, Robert A. F. *The Life and Teachings of Tsong Khapa*. Dharamsala: Library of Tibetan Works and Archives, 1982.

Willis, Janice D. *Enlightened Beings*. Boston: Wisdom Publications, 1995.

Willson, Martin. *Rites and Prayers*. London: Wisdom Publications, 1985.

Willson, Martin. *Shakyamuni Puja*. London: Wisdom Publications, 1988.

About the Author

Geshe Jampa Gyatso was born in Dham in north-central Tibet in early 1932, although his passport has his birthdate as December 15, 1932. The first of seven children of a Tibetan nomad family, he was named Pelgyä by his parents. As an infant he suffered from frequent illnesses that at times even risked his life, but his health dramatically improved when he reached the age of four. During that same year, a visiting Nyingma lama predicted that the boy would leave home at thirteen to become a monk, and would never want for physical nourishment. At the age of seven he received the intermediate renunciate vows from the famed Purchog Jamgon Rinpoche of Sera Je Monastery. Rinpoche, recognized as the manifestation of the future Buddha Maitreya, gave the boy the name 'Jampa Gyatso,' which means 'Ocean of Love.'

Although it wouldn't be until the age of twenty-two that Geshe Jampa Gyatso would become a fully ordained monk, at the age of thirteen he did indeed leave home to live and study at the famous Sera Je Monastery outside Lhasa as predicted nine years earlier. His routine for the next three years was strict: rising at four A.M., he would clean the room and make offerings on the altar before making a fire for tea. At first his time was spent mainly in memorizing texts and helping with chores, though he would sometimes 'escape' for a walk to Lhasa or to a nearby lake.

At sixteen, Jampa Gyatso began his formal study of Buddhist philosophy with the text called *Collected Topics*, memorizing pages while he did his chores. He attended the various daily assemblies of monks in the main hall and began to learn and practice the art of debate, which is used as a means to study and actualize the meaning of the philosophical texts. It was at Sera that Jampa Gyatso met Lama Thubten Yeshe, who would become one of his dearest friends. Jampa Gyatso and Lama Yeshe were ardent debaters, and formed debating groups amongst their friends to practice the art of debate together. When they weren't in class or debating, Jampa Gyatso and Lama

Yeshe, along with another friend, would sneak off to Lama Yeshe's room. There, behind the locked door they would read the songs and biographies of great meditators.

During this time Jampa Gyatso took ordination as a novice monk with the great master, Tag Rig Dorje Chang, studied the vows, and received lam-rim teachings from the tutor of the Dalai Lama. For the next six years he studied the Perfection of Wisdom (*prajñāpāramitā*) sutras and continued to receive teachings on the lam-rim. Encouraged by his guru, Geshe Tashi Bum, at the age of twenty-two Jampa Gyatso received full ordination.

Jampa Gyatso's life took a dramatic turn in 1959 when the Chinese occupation of Tibet forced him, like thousands of other Tibetans, to leave his native land. Leaving his precious texts, sadhanas, and possessions behind, on March 27, 1959, on the advice of his guru, together with Lama Yeshe he joined a party of thirty-five to escape toward Bhutan and eventually on to India. The route was rigorous, and when Jampa Gyatso arrived in Buxa, India, he was very ill. He was immediately admitted to a regional hospital where he remained for five months, then to a larger hospital in Rajastan where he stayed for almost a year and a half.

After nearly two years of hospitalization, in 1961 Jampa Gyatso returned to his studies, this time at the monastic settlement at Buxa. There he continued with six years of study and debate. Then, in 1967, along with fifty other older monks, Jampa Gyatso entered the newly instituted Buddhist studies program at the Sanskrit University in Varanasi to study toward the degree of Acharya, which he received in 1970. Then at the request of the Religious Affairs Department of the Tibetan Government, Jampa Gyatso continued his studies at the Lower Tantric College. One year later, after completing extensive examinations at the three monasteries of Sera, Ganden, and Drepung and having debated in Dharamsala at the annual prayer festival in 1972, he became a lharampa geshe, the highest level awarded.

Geshe Jampa Gyatso spent the next several years helping in the preparation of the land that was donated by the Indian government to the Lower Tantric College. He worked in the field until a request from the Religious Affairs Department petitioned him to leave to take part in a new research program at the Higher Tibetan Institute in Varanasi. With the help of other scholars, Geshe Jampa Gyatso chose to investigate and compare the various interpretations of the aspects of the three knowers (a topic from the Prajñāpāramitā sutras) from the viewpoint of the different philosophical schools. His research at Varanasi culminated in 1976 with a final thesis of 480 pages.

He returned immediately to the Lower Tantric College, where shortly thereafter he received a letter from his old friend, Lama Thubten Yeshe, founder of the Foundation for the Preservation of the Mahayana Tradition (FPMT). For several years, Lama Yeshe had been teaching Buddhism to an ever-increasing number of interested Westerners, and he now solicited Geshe Jampa Gyatso's help by requesting him to travel to the West to teach. Geshe Jampa Gyatso consented. In 1980, after four years of delays and changes in itinerary, he left for Italy where he has been the principal resident teacher and spiritual guide at Istituto Lama Tzong Khapa, one of the largest FPMT centers, ever since.

Wisdom Publications

WISDOM PUBLICATIONS is a non-profit publisher of books on Buddhism, Tibet, and related East-West themes. Our titles are published in appreciation of Buddhism as a living philosophy and with the special commitment to preserve and transmit important works from all the major Buddhist traditions.

If you would like more information or a copy of our mail order catalogue, and to be kept informed about future publications, please write or call us at: 361 Newbury Street, Boston, Massachusetts, 02115, USA; tel: (617) 536-3358; fax: (617) 536-1897.

The Wisdom Trust

As a non-profit publisher, Wisdom is dedicated to the publication of fine Dharma books for the benefit of all sentient beings. We depend upon sponsors in order to publish books like the one you are holding in your hand.

If you would like to make a donation to the Wisdom Trust Fund to help us continue our Dharma work or to receive information about opportunities for planned giving, please write to our Boston office.

Thank you so much.

Wisdom is a non-profit, charitable 501(c)(3) organization and a part of the Foundation for the Preservation of the Mahayana Tradition (FPMT).

The Foundation for the
Preservation of the Mahayana Tradition

The Foundation for the Preservation of the Mahayana Tradition (FPMT) is an international network of Buddhist centers and activities dedicated to the transmission of Mahayana Buddhism as a practiced and living tradition. The FPMT was founded in 1975 by Lama Thubten Yeshe and Lama Thubten Zopa Rinpoche. It is composed of monasteries, retreat centers, communities, publishing houses, and healing centers, all functioning as a means to benefit others. Teachings, such as those presented in this book, are given at many of these centers.

To receive a complete listing of these centers as well as news about the activities throughout this global network, please request a complimentary copy of the MANDALA journal from:

FPMT CENTRAL OFFICE
P. O. Box 1778
Soquel, California 95073

Telephone: (408) 476-8435
Fax: (408) 476-4823.

Care of Dharma Books

Dharma books contain the teachings of the Buddha; they have the power to protect against lower rebirth and to point the way to liberation. Therefore, they should be treated with respect—kept off the floor and places where people sit or walk—and not stepped over. They should be covered or protected for transporting and kept in a high, clean place separate from more "mundane" materials. Other objects should not be placed on top of Dharma books and materials. Licking the fingers to turn pages is considered bad form (and negative karma). If it is necessary to dispose of Dharma materials, they should be burned rather than thrown in the trash. When burning Dharma, first recite OM, AH, HUNG. Then, visualize the letters of the texts (to be burned) absorbing into the AH, and that absorbing into you. After that, you can burn the texts.

These considerations may be kept in mind for Dharma artwork, as well as the written teachings and artwork of other religions.

Also from Wisdom Publications

THE TANTRIC PATH OF PURIFICATION
The Yoga Method of Heruka Vajrasattva
Lama Yeshe

"We have to understand that the qualities of Vajrasattva are already within us. But our realizations, method and wisdom are limited. These have to be developed by our identifying with the limitless pure energy of the archetype. Instead of thinking of ourselves as limited, hopeless sentient beings, we have to recognize our incredible potential. We can free ourselves from the confusion of uncontrolled concepts. We can develop our consciousness to the limitless states of universal compassion, universal love, universal wisdom, universal freedom. The Vajrasattva practice can lead us beyond ego, beyond grasping and beyond the dualistic mind."—Lama Yeshe

In this wonderful book, Lama Thubten Yeshe explains one of the most powerful mental purification practices in the vast array of Buddhist meditations. Included is an entire section of complete retreat instructions—required reading for anybody who undertakes a retreat in the Tibetan tradition.

$15.00, 344 pages, 0-86171-020-7

REINCARNATION
The Boy Lama
Vicki Mackenzie

"The Boy Lama" is the reincarnation of Lama Thubten Yeshe, perhaps the most significant Tibetan lama in the transmission of Tibetan Buddhism to the Western world.

Born in Tibet in 1935, Lama Yeshe became a monk at the age of six. In 1959, he was forced from his homeland into exile in India by the Chinese invasion and began teaching Westerners in 1967. He founded the world-wide Foundation for the Preservation of the Mahayana Tradition (FPMT), which now has more than eighty centers and thousands of students in eighteen countries.

Lama Yeshe passed away in 1984. He was reborn in Spain in 1985 as Lama Tenzin Ösel Rinpoche, and was confirmed by the Dalai Lama the following year. This book tells the remarkable story of Lama Yeshe's life, death, and rebirth, while explaining the controversial phenomenon of reincarnation in a clear, engaging, and practical way.

Vicki Mackenzie is an English journalist who lives in Melbourne, Australia.

$16.95, 228 pages, 0-86171-108-4

CREATION AND COMPLETION
Essential Points of Tantric Meditation
Jamgön Kongtrul Lodrö Thaye

Jamgön Kongtrul Lodrö Thaye, a master practitioner and one of the most prolific writers of eighteenth-century Tibet, composed *Creation and Completion* as a guide to the effective practice of tantric Buddhist meditation. The text leads the way along a clear path of meditative self-transformation; from visualization of oneself in an enlightened form (creation, or generation, stage yoga) to the direct realization of the ultimate nature of reality (completion, or perfection, stage yoga).

These powerful meditation techniques are presented here in Sarah Harding's excellent translation, which includes an extensive introduction to tantric practice. Beginners and experienced meditators alike will benefit from the concise descriptions of the meaning and effect of these once-secret techniques.

"*Creation and Completion* will answer all questions and resolve all doubts about Vajrayana practice, such as 'Why there are deities in a non-theistic tradition?' and 'Why there are such elaborate practices when emptiness is the Mahayana view?'"—Venerable Thrangu Rinpoche

"Sarah Harding has rendered a great service by translating one of Kongtrul's most concise and comprehensive meditation texts."—Ken McLeod, translator of *The Great Path of Awakening*

Sarah Harding is also the author of *Tibetan Language Correspondence Course.*

$14.95, 128 pages, 0-86171-105-X